Songs and Sayings of an Ulster Childhood

By Alice Kane · Edited by Edith Fowke

Songs and Sayings of an Ulster Childhood

WOLFHOUND PRESS

U.K. and Ireland: Publishers
WOLFHOUND PRESS
68 Mountjoy Square
Dublin 1.

ISBN 0 86327 005 0

Typography by The Literary Service, Toronto, Ontario

Printed and bound in Canada by T. H. Best Printing
Company Limited

083498

Credits

The Kipling quotations are printed by permission of
A. P. Watt Ltd. for The National Trust and Macmillan
London Limited.

Pictures on pages 8, 9, and 120 courtesy of the British
Tourist Agency.

Pictures on pages 121 and 151 courtesy of British
Information Services.

Contents

Bangor Harbour, County Down

*A jaunting car beside Carlingford
Lough, County Down*

Introduction

This little book is, I believe, unique. It has many facets: it is a beautiful account of childhood told as through the child's eyes, and it incorporates an amazing amount of different kinds of traditional lore from a group previously poorly recorded: the Ulster Irish. There are other auto- biographies of childhood, and some contain substantial amounts of folklore — Jean Ritchie's *The Singing Family of the Cumberlands* and Dorothy Howard's *Dorothy's World* come to mind, but neither of those incorporates so many different kinds of folklore. There are also other Irish autobiographies of childhood — like Alan Buck's *When I Was a Boy in Ireland* and Robert Harbison's *No Surrender: An Ulster Childhood* — but they contain comparatively little folklore. There are a few collections of Irish children's games and rhymes — notably Collette Hare's *What Do You Feed Your Donkey On*, Eilís Brady's *All In! All In!*, and Maggi Peirce's *Keep the Kettle Boiling*, but these are rhymes given without context. There are also of course many collections of Irish songs, but none encompasses the range of traditional items that Alice remembers. Her narrative has much in common with such books as Flora Thompson's *Lark Rise to Candleford* and Amy Stewart Fraser's *De Ye Min' Langsyne?* which are rich in the folk- lore of English and Scottish children, but they record the folklore of a community rather than of one particular family.

All this wealth of folklore is incorporated in Alice's story of her first thirteen years. Her family moved from Belfast, Northern Ireland, to Saint John, New Brunswick, on Alice's thirteenth birthday, April 18, 1921. For the next few years she spent her winters in New Brunswick and her summers in Montreal, moving in accordance with her father's shipping job. In 1926 she went to McGill where she took an honours course in English and history. Then she came to Toronto where she got a job in the Toronto Public Library and took a librarian's course at the University of Toronto. For forty-three years she worked for the Toronto Public Library, until her retirement in 1973. In the seventies she taught courses in children's literature at the University of New Brunswick in Fredericton, and briefly at Sheridan College in Oakville, and for several years she worked with the Marguerite Bagshaw Puppetry Collection which was set up in memory of a librarian friend.

Today Alice Kane is best known as a storyteller. In 1977 she was one of the founders of the Storytellers School of Toronto, and since then she has been giving classes in storytelling as well as taking part in the "1001 Friday Nights of Storytelling" — weekly open sessions sponsored by the School. She has also helped to plan and participated in the annual Storytelling Festivals that have been held in Toronto since 1979. Dan Yashinsky, another of the School's founders, has acclaimed her "the best story-teller in Canada," and she is kept busy visiting various groups. She has a repertoire of some three hundred stories, most of them fairy tales. Because of her special knowledge of fairy tales, she was asked to translate two of Claude Aubry's French-Canadian tales that were published as *The King of the Thousand Islands* and *The Christmas Wolf*; and later she also translated Aubry's *Le violon magique et autres legendes du Canada français* as *The Magic Fiddler and Other Legends of French Canada*.

I first knew Alice as a children's librarian. When I was preparing the two books of children's lore: *Sally Go Round the Sun* and *Ring Around the Moon*, she gave me rhymes she had learned when she was living in New Brunswick, others she had heard from Toronto children, and some she collected from other librarians. This was the beginning of a close friendship. Every time I saw Alice, she kept coming out with rhymes, songs, and sayings she knew from her childhood, many of which were not familiar to me. I have never met anyone else who had such a vivid memory of early childhood or who had anything like the wealth of songs that float around in Alice's head. Soon I was telling her that she should write them down, that they would be of interest to folklorists. After several years of such exchanges she presented me with a manuscript, "The Songs and Sayings of an Ulster Childhood," as a Christmas present. When I read it I was delighted and excited, for it was not simply a collection of rhymes and songs but a beautifully written narrative incorporating an amazing wealth of folklore: ballads, folk songs, popular songs, music-hall and pantomime songs, sea shanties, hymns, nursery rhymes, children's games, taunts and teases, riddles, recipes, poems, parodies, proverbs, jokes, sayings, and customs. All were presented as she had heard them from her mother, father, aunts, uncles, cousins, and playmates. While many came originally from printed sources — notably the many Kipling songs that were her father's favourites — she reproduced them as she remembered hearing them in childhood, even though she later became familiar with some of them in print. She also manages to convey the child's attitude to the things she heard and sometimes did not understand. The whole gives a vivid picture of what it was like to live in Belfast before and during the First World War.

When Alice gave me her manuscript I began to try to track down as many as possible of her rhymes, songs, and sayings. In the notes that follow her story I give some idea of the background of the various items and indicate where other versions may be found. Of the 390 rhymed quotations listed in the index, I have managed to identify about 350; the remaining ones have so far proved elusive, even though I have consulted many knowledgeable singers and folklorists who I thought might know them. Some are local ditties which probably had very limited distribution, but others I am sure were common in Northern Ireland early in this century. An interesting sidelight is that a considerable number of the songs and rhymes Alice knew were familiar to James Joyce, who incorporated fragments of them in his novels. I have given a list of these following the notes.

Those who helped me to identify some of the items include Tony Barker, Brendan Colgan, Stan Hugill, John Moulden, Tom Munnelly, Iona Opie, Alan Sealey, Hugh Shields, and Michael Yates. I am also grateful to Kenneth Goldstein for the use of his library and for information about some Irish sources.

— Edith Fowke

*Uncles, aunts, cousins
and Mother with Baby Alice*

1. A Chip off the Old Block

I was born on April 18, 1908, at 83 Cedar Avenue in Belfast, County Antrim, Ireland, and christened Alice Elizabeth, after my mother and my maternal grandmother. My birth certificate states that my father was a mariner and my mother's maiden name was Pyper.

My father, Hugh Smiley Kane, was born in Larne, a little market town in County Antrim, at the beginning of the beautiful Coast Road, near the Nine Glens of Antrim where Moira O'Neill wrote *Corrymeela* and near the spot where Robert the Bruce is said to have watched the persevering spider. Until the day he died my father wrote in all his books (*and* some of Mother's) "Hugh S. Kane, Larne," and he asked everyone he met: "Were you ever in Larne?" to which the desired answer was "Hell, man, was I ever out of it?"

John Kane, my grandfather, was a doctor who died in a typhoid epidemic, leaving behind a young widow, Isabella Whiteford, and four little children, not much more than babies: James Whiteford, my Uncle Jim; Hugh Smiley, my father; Thomas Wheeler, my Uncle Tom; and Mary Morgan, my Aunt Mollie. This was before the days of universal insurance so the destitute family was taken in by my grandmother's parents.

We knew very little about our Grandfather Kane. I have a long-ago memory of leaning over a stone bridge in the

15

centre of Larne and being told by a grown-up, maybe Great-Aunt Minnie Whiteford, "That's the Black River that killed your grandfather." Then there was a story about a student celebration which led to his being expelled on the eve of graduation from staid Queen's University and getting his degree instead from a Catholic university in the South, and besides that I saw a mourning ring with a lock of his red hair in it, and a little black-edged card tucked into my father's photograph album saying "In Memoriam, Dr. John Kane, Absent in the Body, Present with the Lord."

Great-Grandfather Whiteford, Granny's father, known to his daughters as Dada, was, I gather, a stern man but basically kind, for the four children were fed and educated and raised most generously. He was a Presbyterian minister in the days of the Church of Ireland establishment and a farm was given to him in lieu of stipend. On it the little Kanes grew up. Besides his memories of butter and eggs, bacon and beef and pork, Daddy spoke with love of the gooseberries which I remember too, big sweet golden ones, little green ones, tart-sweet red ones, ten or twelve kinds.

There was moral food too for growing children. Great-Grandfather and a bevy of aunts provided such truths as:

— "Satan finds some mischief still for idle hands to do."

— "Early to bed, early to rise
  Makes a man healthy, wealthy, and wise."

— "A soft answer turneth away wrath."

— "Save your breath to cool your porridge."

— "Pride goeth before a fall."

— "Tell the truth and shame the devil."

Of these aunts of my father's I only really remember two: Great-Aunt Jane, in whose garden among the gooseberries my cousin Paddy learned to walk; and Great-Aunt Minnie Whiteford, who never married but lived until she died in Larne. There for many summers I went to visit her, looking with love at her plain old face and thinking it the most beautiful in the world. It was at her house that I first saw, tasted, and loved a great wheel of Stilton cheese, and tomato soup with rice (a party treat), and heard such maxims as:

— "Better be sick than waste the good food."

— "Never keep it for yourself, share it with the rest."
(She reinforced this with enough money to go round.)

— "Cheap materials don't last, good ones do."

In my great-grandfather's kitchen at Christmas time the children used to see the mummers, a group of farm hands in their rough costumes and big boots, come to do their Christmas play and collect their Christmas boxes. Before I had even heard the names of St. George or the Turkish Knight or the Dragon himself, I was familiar with the two mercenary characters who closed the play:

Here come I, Beelzebub,
And over my shoulder I carry my club,
And in my hand my frying pan,
And pleased to get all the money I can,

and then there was Little Devil Doubt:

Here come I, Little Devil Doubt.
If you don't give us money

I'll sweep you all out.
Money I lack, money I crave,
If you don't give us money
I'll sweep you to the grave.

These two made a lasting impression on Daddy, and he passed them on to us.

After a few years at Ballyvernston, my grandmother took the two elder boys, Jim and Hugh, up to Belfast with her and they exchanged Larne Grammar School for the Royal Belfast Academical Institution, or Inst, as it was called. Some of my father's great fund of song and sayings and taunts came from the Ballyvernston days in Larne and some from Belfast. Their life, as he remembered it, seemed rough to us, and I often think my Edwardian generation was a tame one compared with theirs.

In the North Irish cold the boys wore knitted mufflers round their necks, and both Daddy and Uncle Jim described to us the gauntlet of their day:

A boy meeting a rival, or group of rivals, tightens his muffler with a defiant air, pulling the two ends. The other side asks: "Who are you tight'nin' your muffler furninst?" And the challenger replies: "I'm tight'nin' it aginst *you*!"

Also from Daddy's Larne/Belfast days:

Boys O boys I found a penny,
Boys O boys I bought a bap.
Boys O boys I ate it up,
Boys O boys it made me fat.

And:

If you weren't so Ballymena
And you had some Ballymoney

You could buy a Ballycastle
To be your Ballyholme.

He also had fragments of enlistment songs and sad army
songs of wars before my time:

Don't take the shilling, lad,
Don't, for Heaven's sake!
Don't take the shilling or
Your mother's heart will break.
You're the only son that's left to me,
Don't let us part.
Don't take the shilling or
You'll break your mother's heart.

(The shilling, from the recruiting sergeant, was an "earnest"
or token, pronounced in Ulster "arnst.")

Another song of war was:

On the banks of the stream stood a lad and his lassie,
The lad's name was Geordie, the lassie's was Jean.
She put her arms round him and said, "Dinna
    leave me,"
But Geordie was gone for to fight for his Queen.

And another, just a scrap, which was to float downstairs
during shaving — it began, I think, on the banks of the
Nile, where:

A brave Irish soldier, a gallant dragoon,
Read his mother's letter by the light of the moon.

When Granny Kane moved to Atlantic Avenue in Belfast
with her elder children, Jim and Hugh, there lived in a big

19

house on the Antrim Road nearby a family called Pyper. The house was named Mount Delphi and it needed to be fairly large, for beside my grandparents, Hugh and Elizabeth Pyper, there were fifteen children! Of these the eleventh was my mother, Alice, and the eighth was Aunt Jennie who married my father's elder brother, my Uncle Jim. A song that I always thought was about them (with some of the names wrong) went like this:

> Tra la la la, I'm father of a family.
> Three small girls and four small boys.
> Jack, John, Jim, Joe, Mary, Jane and Emily —
> Hurrah for matrimonial joys!

My mother's family were very close and devoted to each other, and I really believe they all thought being part of that large warm group was a special mark of favour on the part of Providence. They were self-sufficient in many ways, needing little outside companionship. To me as a child they were a group known as "the uncles" or "the aunts and uncles" or, in my prayers, "God bless all my uncles and aunts and cousins."

By the time I came along in 1908, many of these aunts and uncles had moved away. The two younger Kanes, Uncle Tom and Aunt Mollie, became an actor in New York and a schoolteacher in Liverpool. The other two, my father and Uncle Jim, married two Pyper sisters, Alice and Jennie, so our small cousin Paddy and his sisters were our cousins twice over, and in early childhood our immediate family.

Some of the big Pyper family moved to Canada and the United States or to Dublin or Bangor, out of our immediate field. The ones who were left were the strongest influences of our childhood, along with Mammy and Daddy.

Uncle Toe, whose baptismal name was Hugh but who

called himself in his baby days "Wee Toe Pyter," was the family patriarch. He was unmarried and always seemed to have time for the needs of his sisters and brothers and their children. During "The War" when the other men were away at the front, he organized an evening dancing class for his sisters and those of their husbands who were available, and it was he who taught us the Lancers, Sir Roger de Coverley, waltzes, polkas, and so on in the small drawing room at 15 Hughenden Avenue. (It seemed big to me then.)

Uncle Harry, a bachelor until after we left Ireland, was my mother's brother who lived with us while my father was away at sea. He taught us many songs, stories, and games, and would come out with us on dark winter nights to play that lovely game, "Jack, Jack, Show Your Light," a sort of "Hares and Hounds" with a flashlight in the dark. He wrote in my autograph album:

A wise old owl sat on an oak.
The more he heard, the less he spoke.
The less he spoke, the more he heard.
Why don't you imitate that wise old bird?

And he had an inexhaustible store of rhymes, games, and riddles.

Aunt Jennie and Uncle Jim were so close to us that it is impossible to look at them objectively. With them and their son Paddy (James Whiteford) we sang and told stories and played games of every kind from "Old Maid" to Tiddlywinks (Paddy and my father called each other Big and Little Tiddlywinks). Marjorie was younger again and was still a toddler when we left for Canada.

Aunt Kathleen was our youngest aunt and we thought her very beautiful with her dark hair and big blue eyes. I have early memories of her with her hair still down her back, and later, when I was about ten, I remember every detail of her wedding. Her husband, Uncle Hubert McManus, was one of our dearest uncles who knew songs and stories in the Ulster vernacular as well as in our everyday English. These I have forgotten, but *he* wrote in my autograph album:

> I never got nothin' from nobody no time.
> I never gave nothin' to nobody no time.
> Until I get somethin' from somebody some time
> I'll never give nothin' to nobody no time.

To this day I can't hear a snatch of the music of my childhood or see a film on the Great War or children playing games on the street without seeing them all:

— Aunt Kathleen in pale-pink net over a blue taffeta slip, waltzing — (where?);

— Uncle Toe, tucking pennies in the toes of our shoes and dancing the polka with us to liven a Sunday afternoon;

— Uncle Jim, singing the babies to sleep or playing "The Grand Old Duke of York" and "The Farmer in the Dell" at Christmas parties with Paddy clinging to his hand;

— Aunt Jennie and Mother stirring the plum puddings and making us all take a turn for luck;

— Great-Aunt Minnie Whiteford, a symbol of generosity, love and continuity, welcoming us with food and song.

Children then were born into families. They were given the family names: Alice Elizabeth, Hugh Pyper, James

Whiteford, etc., etc., and they learned the family jokes and riddles and songs and stories.

From "the uncles" came a batch of tongue twisters:

— A tutor who tooted the flute
   Once tutored two tooters to toot.
   Said the two to the tutor
   "Is it harder to toot
   Or to tutor two tutors to toot?"

— Sister Susie sewing shirts for soldiers.

— She sells sea shells on the sea shore.

— Three grey geese in a green field grazing,
   Grey were the geese but green was the grazing.

— The Leith police dismisseth us.

And also rhymes like these:

— If I were a Cassowary
   Living out in Timbuctoo
   I would eat a missionary
   Coat and hat and hymnbook too.

— If I were a night policeman
   You may bet I'd have a lark
   Watching all the spooning couples
   On the benches in the park.

— Barber, barber, shave a pig!
   How many hairs will make a wig?
   Four and twenty, that's enough.
   Give the poor barber a pinch of snuff.

A favourite story of Daddy's was: An old lady, very deaf, came to church carrying that ancient device for the hard of hearing, an ear trumpet. As the usher showed her to a pew he warned her, "One toot and you're oot."

"One toot and you're oot" became one of Daddy's many lessons in manners, and others were:

— Pretend you were out before.

— Toujours la politesse.

— Nous allong à notre bateau nous ne voulons pas un row.

— Remember the Bible text
  And keep your light so shining just
  A little in front of the next.

— As it was in the beginning
  Is today, official sinning,
  And shall be evermore.

— Ah gentle dames it gars me greet
  To think how mony counsels sweet,
  How mony pleasant sage advices
  The husband frae the wife despises.

— It's an old old thing, the wife getting on to me, but that doesna' signify. Last night she said to me, "This drinking business is getting to be a regular habit with you, John." I tell her: "It's no sich thing a habit, wife, it's a . . . it's a . . . it's a Gift!"

— Put your money on the wee gee gees and enjoy your-self.

It's impossible to describe the riches poured on the children of my day. Every grown-up in the family contributed riddle or joke or book or story to inform or amuse or correct. The children passed them on, and here they are as I remember them.

May God bless all my uncles and aunts and cousins and Mammy and Daddy Boy.

*Mother and Alice with assorted
uncles, aunts, and cousins*

Grandfather Kane

Grandmother Pyper

Mother

Daddy

*Feeding the swans
at the Waterworks*

Alice, Hugh, and cousins

Hugh and Alice

2. A Man, a Lady, and a Baby

"Draw me a picture, please" was one of my constant requests as a small child, and to the question "What sort of a picture?" my inevitable reply was: "A Man *and* a Lady *and* a Baby." This was the sum total of my early world, albeit an idealized one for the Man of the picture was a sailor and away for long stretches at sea.

My first real memories are of Mother, whom we called Mammy, mostly shadowy ones and mostly having to do with getting bathed or dressed. A very clear picture is the one of being lifted out of a bath, wrapped in a large towel which covered me from head to foot, and being rubbed vigorously to a cry of: "Where's the baby? Where's the baby?" and finally being extricated to a triumphant: "Och, there she is!"

After the towelling my feet were dried carefully to the rhyme:

> This little piggy went to market,
> This little piggy stayed at home,
> This little piggy had bread and butter,
> But this little piggy had none,
> And *this* little piggy cried "Wee wee wee"
> *All* the way home.

Great-Aunt Minnie Whiteford who lived in Larne was a favourite with all the children of my generation as well as the one before us. She was warm, generous, kind, and good, and full of maxims.

She always did the after-bath drying with a big towel except for the ears and fingers and feet which were gently dried with a soft old red handkerchief. She had a game which she played with the baby's feet. Its meaning is obscure, unless, as I thought long ago, it really is two old drunks seeing each other home:

> This one's Andy Marlin (hold up right foot),
> This one's Tommy Sim (hold up left foot),
> And he bade him to his house (cross over),
> And he bade him (cross over),
> And him and him and him and him and him and him
> and him (feet up and down)
> To mornin', to mornin', to mornin'.

After the baby was all dry it was sung to sleep. Mammy's lullaby was a very sad song which I loved:

> There was a wee lambie fell over a rock
> And when it fell over its leg it was broke,
> And all that the poor little lambie could do
> Was to lie and cry out "Billaloo, billaloo!"

Another bathing memory is of two young aunts bending over me (I *know* they were young because of the big black bows at the napes of their necks), and *their* lullaby was:

> Wingy, wangy,
> Hunky dory,
> Poky lory,
> Wingy, wingy, wang.

This was sung to the tune of "Lord, A Little Band and Lowly," a popular children's hymn of my day to which I knew several sets of words. I was fond of the hymn but I gather a little puzzled by it, for I am reported to have asked Uncle Hugh: "Uncle Toe, let's play 'Lord a little band and lowly.' I'll be the band and you can be the lowly."

As I've said, there were lots of uncles and aunts when I was a baby, and later on there was a little brother and more cousins than I could count. I remember them being sung to sleep in the gathering dusk of a Sunday afternoon. Uncle Jim's children were sung a song about their mother, although I am not sure just how we children knew this:

> Kind, kind and gentle is she,
> Kind is my Mary.
> The tender blossom on the tree
> Could not compare with my Mary.

Sometimes this song changed to another which we found very apt for our family of two sisters married to two brothers. We had no idea what "drifted apart" meant so it was a happy song on the whole and obviously about "olden times":

> Two little girls in blue, lad,
> Two little girls in blue.
> They were sisters, we were brothers,
> We learned to love the two.
> One little girl in blue, lad,
> Won your father's heart,
> Became your mother, I married the other,
> But now we have drifted apart.

The plentiful supply of uncles and aunts to play with us and sing to us was one of the greatest satisfactions of my babyhood. Mammy and all the aunts and uncles knew:

> Mammy, Mammy told me O
> You're the sweetest little baby in the county O.
> I looked in the glass and found it so,
> Just as Mammy told me O.

There were also tickling games like this one played on the palm of a baby's hand:

> Lady, lady in the land
> Bear a tickle in your hand.
> If you laugh or if you smile
> You'll never be a lady's child.

Or the fierce-sounding one which I loved and which always brought delighted giggles:

> Heat the poker hot, hot, hot,
> And *bore* a wee hole in the baby.

Then there were the foot-patting rhymes:

> Diddle diddle dumpling, my son John
> Went to bed with his trousers on.
> One shoe off and the other one on,
> Diddle diddle dumpling, my son John.

Sitting comfortably on a broad avuncular shoe, I would sing:

> "This is the way the baby rides,
> The baby rides, the baby rides.
> This is the way the baby rides
> On a cold and frosty morning."

Or grown-ups and babies all together would dance to:

Brian O'Linn and his wife and his mother
They all went over the bridge together.
The bridge broke down and they all fell in,
"There'll be ground at the bottom," says Brian O'Linn.

Oh Brian O'Linn he hadn't a coat
So he borrowed the skin of an elderly goat.
With the hairy side out and the woolly side in,
"Sure it's pleasant for wearing," says Brian O'Linn.

And Brian O'Linn had no hat for his head
So he borrowed a pot from a neighbour instead.
The pot it did shine for 'twas all made of tin.
"Sure they'll think it is silver," says Brian O'Linn.

When Daddy was coming, the whole house was full of preparation. I can remember the bustle and excitement, but of the actual preparations I can only remember picking pansies from the front garden and learning to play "Clap hands! Daddy's coming home," and:

Dance to your Daddy, my little babby,
Dance to your Daddy, my little man.
You shall have a fishy on a clean dishy,
You shall have a fishy when his ship comes in.

Which was much more cheerful than the usual:

There's nae luck aboot the hoose,
There's nae luck ava'.
There's little pleasure in the hoose
When our gudeman's awa.

Then one day I remember the outline of a man's head in a hat against the front door and the lovely but incomprehensible explanation, "Daddy caught the earlier tide."

Now the house rang with a new kind of song. In the morning to the sound of a razor being stropped came:

"'Tis a famous story, proclaim it far and wide
And let your childeren's childeren re-echo it
   with pride —
How Cardigan the fearless his name immortal made
When he crossed that Russian valley with his famous
   Light Brigade."

Everything was an occasion for a verse or a song or a wild cry of delight or protest. Years later my father's grandson was to remark: *"Grandfather knows a song about everything."* When I came to meet him as an infant learning to walk, with hand outstretched saying politely, "How goo goo goo?" he danced up and down and sang with delight:

"How goo goo goo,
Bunty doodle ido.
Don't you feel like
Standing on your head?

When you're single
You wish that you were married,
And when you're married
You wish that you were dead."

To the end of his days he called me Bunty Doodle Ido (or some part thereof) and always got me lottery tickets under the pseudonym BDI. "How goo goo goo" was one of his constant cries of greeting, but he had sayings to suit every occasion, like "It's a poor heart that never rejoices" or "Life's too short for worrying." A celebration might bring forth a music-hall song like:

> Playing the Game in the West
>   (i.e., the West End, *not* cowboys)
>
> Leading a life that is *thrilling* —
> Out of my two bob piece
> All I've got left's a shilling.
> Treating the girls to cham,   (i.e., champagne)
> Flashing and dashing about,
> I'm not going home till a quarter to ten
> For this is my Night Out.

Instead of the more usual nursery songs, he would shout: "Johnny get your gun and your pistols loaded"; and instead of "Mammy, Mammy told me O," *he* sang:

> "O Patsy you're a villain,
> Patsy, you're a rogue.
> There's nothing o' ye Irish
> Except your name and brogue.
> You're killing me by inches,
> You're making me your slave.

And a request for a ride on his foot brought:

> "All the girls declare he's a gay old stager.
> Hi! Hi! clear the way — here comes the galloping
>   major."

Besides his lusty songs of the sea or the music halls, Daddy knew many nursery rhymes and interspersed them with Kipling's *Just So* verses in a glorious never-to-be-forgotten medley. The chief characteristic of all his singing was exuberance. He was always off-key and when he forgot a word he substituted another, but the rhythm was strong and true and everything was full of vitality. He could raise questions about the meaning or provide parodies for almost everything. I remember (or I *think* I remember; I may have been told) a long argument one morning between my father, still in bed, and my little brother on the bed beside him. They were chanting together the story of Mary's little lamb until they came to:

> "The teacher therefore turned it out,
> Turned it out, turned it out,
> The teacher therefore turned it out
> But still it lingered near
> And waited patient-lally bout."

> "*No*, laily bout."
> "Lally bout."
> "Laily bout."

The argument went on until not Mary but Mammy appeared to announce breakfast, when Daddy switched to:

> "Mary had a little lamb.
> The lamb and she have long been dead.
> If Mary were alive again
> She'd have an aeroplane instead."

And then Mammy gave us:

> "Mary had a little lamb,
> Its fleece was white as snow,
> And everywhere that Mary went
> She shoved it through the window,"

and we all sang together:

> "The window, the window,
> She shoved it through the window.
> If you don't watch what you're about
> We'll shove you through the window."

There were not many dull moments when Daddy was home. Once (before I was three) he carried me in the rain down to the grocery store of Mr. Alexander on Cavehill Road. It was a wobbly ride high up under a big umbrella but typical of the larger horizons that life had to offer when the Man came home to join the Lady and the Baby.

> So merry, so merry, so merry are we,
> There's none like a sailor that sails on the sea.
> Blow high, blow low as the ship glides along,
> Give a sailor his grog and there'll nothing go wrong.

3. Our Daily Bread

"Give us a piece, Mammy"

Family parties, summer picnics, festivals like Christmas
and Easter and birthdays all have their traditional foods.
The staples of my childhood diet were simple and, for the
most part, local. Those were not the days of imported
strawberries in the dead of winter or strange exotic vegetables. We waited for the strawberry season, our fish came
fresh that morning from the sea, our eggs were new-laid,
and it never seemed monotonous to us.

Porridge ushered in the day, eaten in large soup plates,
and invariably greeted by Daddy, if he was at home, with:

"A rowdledy dowdledy, porridge and milk,
A rowdledy dowdledy, stir them up thick,
A rowdledy dowdledy, taste on the spoon,
A rowdledy dowdledy, blow till they cool."

Porridge was usually oatmeal, and Daddy always referred
to it in the plural. Mammy did not care for this: she was a
townswoman and that was not the way they spoke. We
were never offered sugar on it but it was well salted, and
like children everywhere we made canals and tunnels
through it until we were told, "Eat up your porridge. It
will stick to your ribs."

Bread appeared at the evening meal and was, in fact, the main item on the menu. It was nearly always home-made, not baked, mind you, but cooked on a big griddle on top of the stove. This was one of the things I learned to make; it is very easy and my mother's recipe went like this:

1½ lbs of flour
½ pint of buttermilk
1 teaspoon of baking soda
1 teaspoon of salt
   Turn out on a floured board, roll to one-inch
   thickness, cut into four quarters (known as farls)
   and bake on the griddle, turning once.

Newly baked soda bread was pure heaven, split while still warm, buttered and spread with strawberry jam, or even blackberry or damson. This was the everyday snack of Ulster children and they asked as they came through the door: "Give us a piece, Mammy." One child I knew thought that the Lord's Prayer contained a request for the perpetual provision of this piece. Wheaten bread (a version of soda bread made with whole wheat flour) was also cooked at home on the griddle or sometimes in the oven, and Fadge or potato bread was a griddle delicacy also.

In our house baker's bread was more or less of a rarity and my little brother and I called it "fancy bread," much to the astonishment of some of my mother's guests. Fancy bread was used for sandwiches and for ladies' tea parties when it was cut almost paper-thin, buttered, and eaten by ladies balancing cups of tea, who lifted it delicately, turned it over double with a quick turn of the wrist, and ate it in small bites with their veils rolled above their nose tips and their fingers coming out of unbuttoned gloves. These tea parties (always held while Daddy was away at sea) amused him very much and he had a song of which I can only remember a scrap. It was about a tea party to which he was bidden by a "pretty gilt-edged invitation" so he "went just for old friendship's sake" and he was offered a slice of Miss Fogarty's beautiful cake:

> There was plums, prunes, cherries,
> Blackberries and cinnamon too;
> There was caraway seeds and blayberries
> And the crust it was stuck on with glue.
> There was sugar and peel in abundance
> Built up for a fine stomachache —
> It would kill a man twice after eating a slice
> Of Miss Fogarty's beautiful cake.

Bakers' bread, the kind we called fancy bread, was delivered fresh every day by the Ormeau Bakery (which still exists and sells to Canada). The baker's man was called by us children "Billy-a-Bun" and we loved a ride on his cart.

Besides "fancy bread" Billy-a-Bun brought us such dainties as fruit loaf and the very special fruit loaf of Hallowe'en, known as Barm Brack. It was welcome not only for its raisins and spice but for the treats hidden away inside in little twists of paper. Hallowe'en was a great fortune-telling time in Ulster and these miniatures had a significance for the grown-up that we did not understand. To us children a little thimble or a silvery button was just as welcome as a ring or a three-penny bit. Oh, yes, and Billy brought baps, those wonderful chewy buns brushed with sugar of which all Ulster children sang:

> "My Aunt Jane she called me in,
> She gave me tea in her wee tin.
> Half a bap with sugar on the top,
> And three black lumps from her wee shop."

Everyone knows that the staple food of Ireland is the potato, just as everyone has heard of the Irish potato famine which helped to populate the western world. We loved potatoes which were treated reverently and properly cooked. No greasy French fries for us, no English potatoes peeled and soaked in cold water. Proper Irish potatoes kept their skins decently on while they cooked and were served "with a stone at the heart" — never mushy. The best ones were those which cracked their skins as they cooked, split their sides laughing in fact, so that our mother used to say, "Here's a lovely big laughing one for you."

Sometimes in the spring our potatoes *were* peeled, and this was to make champ. Champ was a child's delight, potatoes lightly mashed (beetled) with hot milk, seasoned with salt and pepper and scallions, served in big soup plates, and eaten with a spoon, a spoon that pushed the potatoes in from the edge to the lovely melting butter in the middle. This was champ and it was served with a glass of buttermilk on the side. One summer I was down at Ballycarry for the haymaking and I was told that one allowed a quarter stone of potatoes for champ and a pint of buttermilk for each haymaker. Favourite of children and haymakers, this was also the theme of a nursery song:

> There was an old woman who lived in a lamp.
> She hadn't no room to beetle her champ
> So she up with her beetle and broke the lamp
> And then she had room to beetle her champ.

(And that reminds me of another verse about an old woman that I learned from Mother:

> There was an old woman who lived in a sink.
> She lived upon nothing but victuals and drink.
> Victuals and drink was the whole of her diet
> And this poor old woman could never be quiet.)

In Ireland, potatoes were, of course, something else, something symbolic. Great-Aunt Minnie Whiteford, whose memory went back a long way, used to stop sometimes and look at the table and say, "Thank God for the good potatoes." After we came to Canada, I remember my father complaining that you couldn't get a decent potato in this country at all. "But Daddy," we protested, "this is where potatoes come from." "Oh, yes," he told us, "I grant you *that* — but look what the Irish have made of the North American yam." And then he sang to us, strong and clear:

"When the Queen wants a man to fight wi' her foes
It's no' to her rabid devourers she goes
But awa' to the land of the brave and the darin',
The lads that were bred upon tatties and herrin'."

And in spite of our convictions and the unfairness of the argument, we joined in the chorus:

"Tatties and herrin', boys, tatties and herrin',
The lads that were bred upon tatties and herrin'."

Mother was fairer and less boisterous, and she taught us:

The potatoes they grow small over there,
The potatoes they grow small over there.
The potatoes they grow small and they plant them
    in the fall
And they eat them skin and all over there.

At Christmas we *really* feasted. Aunt Jennie had a big old house downtown and after we had opened our stockings and forced some breakfast down, we went to Aunt Jennie's for dinner. The tramcars were off for the holiday, so the Station Cab Company sent a vehicle, booked well in advance, to take us to Great Victoria Street. Sometimes it was a taxi; motorcars were rare and a treat to us; and sometimes it was a sidecar, known in song as a jaunting car. We never could decide which we liked best: the taxi, so shiny, so modern, but so terribly fast, or the more leisurely old-fashioned sidecar, clip-clopping through the empty streets. We knew several songs about jaunting cars:

> Do you want a car, Your Honour, och sure that's
> the one for you,
> It's an outside Irish jaunting car all painted green
> and blue.
> It belongs to Larry Doolan and you'll have to travel
> far
> To find a better driver of an Irish jaunting car.
> The fare is fifteen pence but as the distance isn't far
> I'll just say one and threepence, sir, so jump upon
> my car.

> If you want to drive round Dublin, sure you'll find
> me on the Strand.
> I'll take you to the Phoenix Park, to Nancy's Hands,
> and then
> I'll take you to the Strawberry Beds and back to
> town again.
> Get some ale and beer and porter and some whiskey
> in a jar —
> That's the way to take your pleasure on an Irish
> jaunting car.

> When the Queen was here in Dublin sure she wished
> her health to thrive
> And the darlin' Duke of Leinster thought he'd take
> her for a drive,
> So she jumped on his outsider, but before they had
> gone far,

> "Och," says she, "I like the jolting of your Irish
>   jaunting car."
> So she got one made in Dublin and she wrote to
>   Mr. Mehar
> To send her Larry Doolan to drive her jaunting car.

When we arrived at Aunt Jennie's it was festive indeed. Uncles and aunts and cousins from near and far had come from Belfast and Larne and Bangor, Dublin, and even England. Presents were exchanged and the children ran up and down stairs, opened parcels, played all manner of games, and sneaked sweeties before dinner, and occasionally stole downstairs to the kitchen to see how things were coming along. In Irish fashion the enormous turkey was always accompanied by a big ham, covered with mustard and buttered breadcrumbs, and stuck with cloves, as well as bacon and strings of plump little pork sausages. (Fowl alone was not considered much of a dinner.) Also, there was always bread sauce and riced potatoes and vegetables and then the wonderful rich satisfying dessert to complete the feast: plum pudding and mince pie and apples and nuts and muscatel raisins.

Months before when the plum pudding and mincemeat were being made, every child in the household, and some of the grown-ups, came down to the kitchen to help by giving a stir to the mixture. This was for luck and it went with the songs and rhymes we began to say in November as the puddings were started. One was a riddle:

> Flour of England, fruit of Spain
> Met together in a shower of rain;
> Put in a bag, tie up with string,
> If you tell me this riddle I'll give you a ring.

The answer, of course, is a plum pudding. There were also

King Arthur's plum pudding, which the Queen next morning fried, and the Christmas pie of Little Jack Horner. We knew about half of the familiar carols of today and songs like "Christmas is Coming, the Goose is Getting Fat," and the silly one about the spineless child who couldn't even choose her own Christmas present:

> As for me, my little brain isn't very bright.
> Choose for me, old Santy Claus, what you think
>   is right.

Like chicken or turkey which needed ham or sausages to make them palatable, fish was not a favourite of my father's. Lobster, prawns, shrimps, salmon, or even finnan haddie or Bismarck herring were all right, but plain fish, baked or fried, was apt to be greeted with his abominable French: "Voulez-vous du *poison*, Mademoiselle?" or one of his many loud cries: "Pork and peas as much as you please but no more of your cod, Mrs. Murphy, or I leave your house in the morning." He had, however, a number of rhymes about fish which made it apparent that, liked or not, fish was a staple food of the country. Some that I remember are:

> Sally Walker sells fish,
> Three ha'pence a dish.
> Cut the heads off,
> Cut the tails off,
> Sally Walker sells fish.

And two, frequently sung by both parents:

> In Dublin's fair city
> Where the girls are so pretty
> I first set my eyes on sweet Molly Malone.

She wheeled her wheelbarrow
Through streets broad and narrow
Crying "Cockles and mussels, alive, alive O!"

She was a fishmonger
And sure 'twas no wonder
For so was her father and mother before.
They both wheeled their barrow
Through streets broad and narrow
Crying "Cockles and mussels, alive, alive O!"

She died of a fever
And nothing could save her
And that was the end of sweet Molly Malone,
But her ghost wheels her barrow
Through streets broad and narrow
Crying "Cockles and mussels, alive, alive O!"

Alive, alive O! Alive, alive O!
Crying "Cockles and mussels, alive, alive O!"

or:

Buy my caller herrin',
They're bonny fish and halesome farin',
Buy my caller herrin'
New drawn from the Forth.

Then there was the little rhyme:

One, two, three,
Mother caught a flea.
We roasted it and toasted it
And had it to our tea.

And the chant for shaking the tablecloth that had been spread on the ground for a picnic:

> Toss the blanket, toss the blanket,
> Turn the blanket over.

Mother and Aunt Kathleen had a special rhyme for guests:

> Th'art as welcome, just as welcome as can be,
> Th'art welcome, just as welcome as can be.
> Draw thy chair up to the fire,
> Stay as long as thou desire,
> For we're always glad to see a man like thee.
>
> Th'art as welcome, just as welcome as can be,
> Th'art as welcome, just as welcome as can be.
> Draw thy chair up to the table,
> Eat as much as thou art able,
> For we're always glad to see a man like thee.

The real treat in the food line was, of course, "sweeties." To children of a war and a sugar shortage candy of any kind was expensive, scarce, and highly prized. Ladies went out to tea parties carrying their own two lumps of sugar in little silver boxes. Hard candies like aniseed balls (the black lumps of Aunt Jane's wee shop) or humbugs doubled in price. At the fairs in Larne or Ballycastle the yellowman (a sort of sponge toffee) was yellow all right but bitter and barely candy at all, and the cry:

> Treat your Mary Anne
> To some dulse and yellowman

lost its magic. I liked to play at being Princess Marie of the

Belgians; I had often seen pictures of her in a short white frock reviewing the troops with her father, and she was a romantic figure to me. I was sure *she* didn't have porridge for breakfast but probably a lovely confection I knew called Whipped Cream Walnuts, a beehive of milk chocolate with fluffy cream filling and a big walnut on top. Tuppence ha'penny apiece they cost, and I could hardly ever afford even one, but a princess could probably have two or more any time she chose. When Daddy came home though, *he* showered us with many favourites: Dolly Mixture, a poke of Cadbury's Dorothy chocolates, licorice allsorts, sugared almonds, even Clarnico marzipan. Mother, less prodigal, would put her hands behind her back and call upon us to choose:

> "Neevy, neevy, nick nack,
> Which hand will you tak'?
> Tak' the right, tak' the wrang,
> I'll beguile you if I can."

But somehow we always guessed right!

One of the paraphrases of my Sunday School days says in praise of Wisdom:

> The young She leads with innocence
> In Pleasure's paths to tread,
> A crown of glory She bestows
> On every hoary head.

I often think of this now that *my* head is hoary, for another persistent memory from my earliest days is of Mammy saying, as she laid a sweetie on my tongue:

> "Open your mouth and shut your eyes
> And I'll give you something to make you wise."

4. Watch for Bicycles

Every morning Mother came with me to the front door, checked that I had my schoolbag, my handkerchief, two Marie biscuits for recess, and a penny for emergencies, warned me to watch for bicycles, kissed me good-bye, and sent me off to school. At the end of a very short walk was the school, run by three gentle Quaker ladies: Miss Margaret Hanna, and her sisters, Miss Lydia and Miss Bertha. At home I was spanked occasionally, called names like "Tory Rogue" (in a Whig country), "Farden Face" (when I was not looking well), or even "Dog in the Manger." Occasionally I was invited to shake hands with an uncle or other adult with the words:

"Shake hands, Brother,
You're a rogue and I'm another."

At school no hard word was ever said to us, let alone a hand raised in anger, but between the safety of home and the secure peace of school lay a hazardous way, full of strange children and an unknown language. These children, my contemporaries or thereabouts, would stop in their tracks, look at me, and call, "Speckled four eyes, old speckled four eyes." At first I didn't understand this at all.

Then I learned it had to do with my glasses, and misery overwhelmed me. However, that wasn't all. Just as I became more or less accustomed to my four eyes, a new taunt met me:

> "Ginger, you're balmy,
> So is your Mammy."

And that was much worse because I couldn't even tell Mammy about it.

The next name I remember being called was Freckles, but at least I had heard that one at home along with Farden Face and Tory Rogue, but I was still hurt and puzzled by it until one day I heard a taunt being thrown at another: "Hello, Fatty," and then to a boy in a bright new suit came the shout: "Hello, Jimmy, where did you get the shorty longs?"

So it happened to everybody! Redheads, spectacles, fat or skinny or freckled, little boys with girlish curls, no one was exempt! Now all I had to do was to learn some taunts myself and get the courage to use them. However, before I did that I had learned to read and write, and with that came a sudden sense of identity. Now *I* could write on sidewalks and proclaim my presence here:

> Alice Kane is my name,
> Ireland is my nation,
> Belfast is my dwelling place,
> And school's my occupation,

or sometimes the whole thing:

> Alice Elizabeth Kane
> 15 Hughenden Avenue
> Belfast

Co. Antrim
Ulster
Ireland
Europe
The World
Space.

And once or twice I wrote out one that I really liked:

Fools' names
Like their faces
Always seen
In public places,

followed by my whole name and address. Now I belonged!
Now I knew what to write and what to say; now I could
boast and pass social and moral judgements on other
children:

Cry, baby, cry,
Stick your finger in your eye,
Tell your mother it was I,
Cry, baby, cry.

Or:

Cowardy, cowardy custard
Had to run for mustard.

Or even that most withering of all our taunts: "Does your
Mammy know you're out?"

Next I learned the games, the innocent questions with
the trick answers for the unwary. At home there was "Put
your finger in the Crow's nest, Crow's not at home"; and
when I put my finger in, Crow came back and pinched me

— very gently, the pinch of a loving grown-up to a child. On the street I was asked:

"Adam and Eve and Pinch Me Tight
Went down to the sea to bathe.
Adam and Eve were drowned —
Which of the three was saved?"

Almost before the words were out of my mouth, the hard pinch came. And then there was the one when you were told to respond "Just like me" to everything your tormentor said:

I went into the house. — Just like me.
I went upstairs. — Just like me.
I went into a room. — Just like me.
I looked in the glass. — Just like me.
I saw a monkey. — Just like me.
Yah! Yah! Yah!

There was a party game too in which dozens of little boys and girls in their best clothes knelt on the floor, bent their foreheads to the ground, and repeated faster and faster the Siamese National Anthem, "Oh, Watanna Siam, Oh, Watanna Siam."

Riddles, of course, pervaded our whole lives. At Sunday School there was Samson and the Lion or Solomon choosing the babies; at school there was King John and the Abbot of Canterbury and the Riddle of the Sphinx. And parents and uncles and aunts and grown-up cousins had old-fashioned riddles which they had known long ago:

— Why does Mr. Gladstone wear red suspenders? — To keep his trousers up.

— Can February March? — No, but April May.

— Do you know the story of the empty jug? — There's nothing in it.

— Do you know the story of the three eggs? — Too bad.

— Why does the donkey eat thistles? — Because he's an ass.

— Why does the chicken cross the road? — To get to the other side.

— Why did the razorbill raise her bill? — To let the sea urchin see her chin.

— Why is the sun like a loaf of bread? — Because it rises in the yeast and sets in the vest.

— Why need you never be hungry in bed? — You can always take two rolls and a turnover.

— Charles the First walked and talked ten minutes after his head was cut off. — Add a semicolon after talked.

— Moses was the son of Pharoah's daughter. He was also the daughter of Pharoah's son. — Hyphenate: daughter-of-Pharoah's son.

— Brothers and sisters have I none
But this man's father is my father's son. — He is my son.

— Londonderry, Cork and Kerry,
Spell me that without a K. — T-H-A-T.

— Robin-a-Bower has broken his band,
   He comes roarin' up the land.
   The King of Scots wi' all his power
   Couldn't stop bold Robin-a-Bower. — The wind.

Adult Questioner (Mammy): What are the resemblances
   among a sheet of foolscap, an inclined plane, a lazy
   young dog, and a pot of glue?
Small Child: I give up.
Adult Questioner: A sheet of foolscap is an ink-lined
   plane; an inclined plane is a slope up; a slow pup is a
   lazy dog.
Small Child: And the pot of glue?
Adult (triumphantly): That's where *you* got stuck.

Adult Questioner: What are the resemblances among the
   Prince of Wales, the bald-headed man, the monkey,
   and the glue pot?
Small Child: I give up.
Adult: The Prince of Wales is the Heir Apparent; the
   bald-headed man has no hair apparent; and the
   monkey has a hairy parent.
   And of course, The Glue Pot.

These were home riddles which had come down from a
long time ago. In fact we were told that Aunt Emily, when
she was our age, had always given the answer to "Can February March?" as "No, but April and May can."

The riddles on the street sometimes included some of
these but also had more up-to-date ones and rude ones
only half understood.

   A big fat German and a little fat German.
   The little fat German is the son of the big fat German
   But the big fat German is not the father of the little
      fat German.

The answer, of course, is that she is his mother.

Rude street ones were:

> Why did the rose blush? — Because she found herself
> in bed with Sweet William.

> Why did the lobster blush? — Because he saw the
> salad dressing.

And Daddy had one which contained a word absolutely
forbidden and therefore *Lovely*!

> What is the difference between a train coming out of
> a tunnel and a lady coming out of a bath?

> — The train comes out with a bloody rush and the
> lady comes out with a ruddy blush.

> *"Don't tell your Mammy."*

Now looking back after more than sixty years I see the
age-old progress of the fledgling from the nest, the prelim-
inary rejection, the beginning of acceptance, and at last the
joyous chauvinism of one's own group. I understood a
little of this long, long ago the day I met the Boy Scout
troop from Ballywalter on a visit to Belfast. They were on
their way home, marching to the station, very tired and a
little defiant, and they sang:

> "It's a long way to Ballywalter,
> It's a long way to go.
> It's a long way to Ballywalter,
> Sweetest place I know.
> *Good*-bye, rotten *Bel*fast,
> Farewell, Shaftesbury Square.
> It's a long, long way to Ballywalter
> But my heart's right there."

5. Pro Tanto Quid

Nowadays when I look back at school it means two different things to me: the actual school, small, serene, and full of interest, where I spent my mornings; and another totally different school which I met in songs and books and in the stories of my parents and playmates.

In the first, the real school, I was taught to read out of the 27th psalm. I learned a tremendous amount of scripture and a wide range of literature, French, Dalcroze eurythmics, and a smattering of mathematics and music. Much of it still remains with me, particularly the text which was so constantly held before us: "Be ye kind one to another, tender-hearted, forgiving one another," and also a puzzling ceremony in the early morning at which each child's name was called and he or she responded with a request for a gift: "Present, please, Miss Hanna" — but the request was never granted.

The other school, at once fascinating and terrifying, was presented partly by my parents and partly by the stories of children I met. Daddy's school was, fortunately, a boys' school, and I would never have to face the terrors of: "Stand up, sir. Leave the room, sir. Don't talk to me, sir!" or "The way was long, the wind was *what*, McGarrett?"

It was Daddy also who recommended that I put a couple of exercise books into my little lace-trimmed drawers so that I wouldn't feel the cane. (Fortunately, Mammy corrected this misapprehension before I set off for Miss Hanna's gentle texts.) *And* it was Daddy who explained the routine for examinations: "Ask Mammy Boy for an ice bag for your head and a hot bottle for your feet."

"Oh and Doodle, if they ever give you a hundred lines, try 'The Prisoner of Chillon'; it's the shortest:

> My hair is white
> But not with years,
> Nor grew it white
> In a single night
> As men's have done
> From sudden fears."

I was, you see, prepared for any eventuality, but I never met any of them.

Curiously, none of this seems to have broken my father's spirit; instead it gave him a lot to sing about and an abiding respect for a headmaster called R. M. Jones.

Mother's stories of her school days were quite different, and most of her memories which she passed on to us were of Infant School. School life to her later on was apparently too serious for song and story, but here are some of her memories of Infant School in the 1880s:

> We're all nodding, nid nid nodding,
> Oh we're all nodding in our pretty Infant School.
> Nod goes one head and another one too,
> Down go our hands, little work we can do,
> For we're all nodding, nid nid nodding,
> Oh we're all nodding in our pretty Infant School.

The next one is very virtuous:

> It's very kind of Teacher
> To take such pains with me.
> I'll show her how attentive
> And obedi-ent I can be.
> And I won't be a Dunce,
> No, I won't be a Dunce —
> I am so fond of learning
> That I cannot be a Dunce.

There were two about workmen of which I only know scraps. One of these stressed "For Father works so hard for me that I'll work hard for him," and there was a merry ditty about "Joe the Railway Porter."

Then there was one which I loved and which was confused with another favourite, Wordsworth's "The Rainbow," with its amazing statement that "The child is father of the man." This one was simple, though:

> A fair little girl sat under a tree
> Sewing as long as her eyes could see.
> Then she smoothed her work and folded it right
> And said, "Dear work, goodnight, goodnight."
>
> A number of rooks flew over her head
> Crying "Caw, caw" on their way to bed.
> She said as she watched their curious flight,
> "Little black things, goodnight, goodnight."

Besides the real school and these pictures of my parents, there was a large collection of songs and anecdotes, riddles and sayings, which illuminated the whole picture of school, school real and imaginary, school past and present, but nearly always with the idea that among one's peers one did not confess to *liking* school. A holiday was always welcome even if there was nothing particular to do. Because of this, Teachers always seemed to be pictured in a way at odds with the characters of Miss Bertha, Miss Lydia, and Miss Margaret.

Teachers

I first gave consideration to the subject of Teachers when, at the tender age of about seven, I was faced with a week-end composition given out to the whole school on the subject "My Ideal Schoolmaster." This was to be based, along with another a few weeks later on "My Ideal Minister," on character sketches in "The Deserted Village" which the whole school, except the real babies in kindergarten, was studying. Here then, as I remember them after sixty-five years, are the ideas on Goldsmith's schoolmaster:

> And still they gazed and still the wonder grew
> How one small head could carry all he knew.
> . . . .
> Lands he could measure, terms and tides presage,
> And e'en the story ran that he could gauge.

Rudyard Kipling in *Stalky and Co.* has presented us with another old-fashioned schoolmaster, the forthright no-nonsense type who prepared his pupils for the battle of life:

> Let us now praise famous men,
> Ancients of the College,
> For they taught us common sense,

Tried to teach us common sense,
Truth and God's own common sense,
Which is more than knowledge,

or:

Bless and praise we famous men
Set in office o'er us,
For they beat on us with rods,
Daily beat on us with rods,
Faithfully with many rods,
For the love they bore us.

To a child who had never seen a school beating, this was very funny. And, of course, in the nursery rhymes there was that beating master:

Dr. Foster was a good man,
He whipped his scholars now and then,
Out of England into France,
Out of Germany into Spain,
Whipped them all in a merry dance,
And then he whipped them home again.

Mathematics

With these vast stores of knowledge and the whip to enforce it all, what did these paragons teach? Mathematics, of course, so that one could do accounts and count change at the market. Unlike today's children with their computers, we were drilled and drilled again in "Tables." Daddy as usual brightened our lot with a song sung to the tune of "Yankee Doodle":

"Five times five is twenty-five,
Five times six is thirty,
Five times seven is thirty-five,
And five times eight is forty."

My little brother came home from school one day at
noon with the proud boast that he was "top in mentals,"
which meant that he had done well in that nerve-wracking
test called mental arithmetic. It was like a spelling bee
except that I loved spelling. Everyone but me seemed able
to do that puzzle where the questioner started: "Take a
number, double it, add ten to it, divide by two, etc., etc.,
etc.," and then miraculously, "Take away the number you
first thought of and the answer is———."
Mother Goose shared my views on mathematics with the
verse:

Multiplication is a vexation,
Division's twice as bad.
The rule of three perplexes me
And practice drives me mad.

Then there was a poem recited by Mother with many
memory gaps (I think it was by Jean Ingelow) which went
in part:

There's no dew left on the daisies and clover,
There's no rain left in Heaven.
I've said my seven times over and over,
Seven times one is seven.

I'm old, so old I can write a letter,
Childhood's nearly done.

The lambs play always, they know no better,
They're only one times one.

A few years later I was to meet Wordsworth's stubborn
child with her reiterated "O Master, we are seven," but I
liked Jean Ingelow better.

We skipped to (but never let Mammy hear):

One two three four five six seven,
All good children go to Heaven.
When they get there hear them yell
All bad children go to hell.

I also had a child's alphabet which assured me that:

Babes can count up by Algebra
All the stripes upon a Zebra.

And, of course, there were riddles like "A man had
twenty sick sheep and one died; how many were left?"
The answer is nineteen but we cheated on this if the
guesser was right and claimed to have said twenty-six.

And for those who are top in mentals there is always:

As I was going to St. Ives
I met a man with seven wives.
Each wife had seven sacks,
Each sack had seven cats.
Each cat had seven kits,
Kits, cats, sacks, and wives,
How many were going to St. Ives?

Serves you right if you did all that arithmetic because I
was the only one going to St. Ives.

French

Now this was really fun, just play, in fact, but in another
secret language. We solemnly planted cabbages à la mode
de chez nous or danced on the bridge at Avignon or
beseeched an unfeeling neighbour for a pen and a light.
We also assured the world that we had plenty of good
tobacco but weren't giving it away, but when we told
Uncle Hubert about this he taught us in return:

> The man who has plenty of good tobacco (or peanuts,
>   or good ripe oranges or strawberry shortcake)
> And giveth his neighbour none,
> He shan't have any of my tobacco
> When his tobacco is done.

Even mathematics in French was fun:

> Un, deux, trois, j'irai dans le bois.
> Quatre, cinq, six, cuellir des cerises.
> Sept, huit, neuf, dans mon pannier neuf.
> Dix, onze, douze, elles sont toutes rouges.

Mother replied with:

> "One, two, buckle my shoe,
> Three, four, shut the door.
> Five, six, pick up sticks.
> Seven, eight, lay them straight.
> Nine, ten, a big fat hen.
> Eleven, twelve, dig and delve.
> Thirteen, fourteen, maids a-courting.
> Fifteen, sixteen, maids a-stitching.
> Seventeen, eighteen, maids a-waiting.
> Nineteen, twenty, MY PLATE'S EMPTY."

And Aunt Kathleen produced:

"One two three four,
Mary at the cottage door
Eating plums off a plate,
Five six seven eight."

In French too there were magic words, and "Il y avait une fois" meant a story and generally a really good one like "Cendrillon" or "Le Petit Chaperon Rouge" or "Le Petit Poucet" or even "La Belle au Bois Dormant," and that was when I first saw the difference in languages for the French *wood* slept while our Princess slept!

When we went home with the French we had learned at school we usually fell upon real riches, not just corresponding English rhymes like the one that greeted "J'ai du bon tabac" or "Un, deux, trois," but the French riddles and songs of Mother's childhood long, long ago. There was a good tongue twister which I have forgotten, and a riddle which asked "What two towns in France are like a sailor's trousers?" (Toulon and Toulouse). Daddy would produce one of his stirring cries of "Toujours la politesse" or "Ils ne passeront pas" or even "Baisez-moi!" or "Toute suite and the tooter the sweeter," or burst into song with:

"Oh Boney was a warrior,
Jean François!
A warrior and a terrier,
Jean François!"

or:

"Bonjour, ma chèrie
And how the hell are you?
Bonjour, ma chèrie,
Comment vous portez-vous?"

(Sometimes he said: "Combien, ma chèrie," but neither Mother nor the children understood this one.)

These, coupled with the "Marseillaise" and some of the more vulgar wartime songs like "Mademoiselle from Armentières," rounded out the more formal teaching of school. However, the song we really loved but mourn the fact that it was incomplete then and is even more scrappy now is the one about Killaloe:

> Now I happened to get born just the time they cut
>   the corn
> Quite contagious to the town of Killaloe,
> And a Frenchy m'sieu came to instruct us in the game,
> To instruct us in the game of Parlez-voo.
>
> You may talk about Descarty, Napoleon Bonaparty,
> Or any other party from "Comment vous portez-voo."
> Och I learned to sing it aisy, that song the
>   Marseillaisy,
> Comment, Boulogne, the Continong, I learned
>   at Killaloe.

The song goes on to relate the adventures of the Boy from County Clare who heard his mother called a mare and the narrator who was assured that he had not one father but a pair. Both retaliated violently to our intense delight:

> "Now send for Johnny Darm," cried M'sieu in alarm.
> Says I, "There's no such name about the place."
> "Comment?" he made reply. "Och, come on
>   yourself," says I,
> And I hit him in what served him for a face.

What *I* learned at Killaloe certainly enriched my life.

Latin

Latin is a dead language,
Dead as dead can be.
First it killed the Romans
And now it's killing me.

The real mystery of Latin seems to be why we ever had to learn it. My mother insisted it was so that we could speak English (and now that nobody learns Latin or speaks English I am inclined to agree with her). My teachers insisted that if it did nothing else it trained my mind. From the first it certainly presented me with puzzles. I had just got over the morning struggle with "Present, please, Miss Hanna" when I was presented with the correct way to address a table. This was called the Vocative Case and it seemed to make sense to teachers and to Mother but to me it was equivalent to Alice's adventure with the joint . . . does one eat the joint to which one has been introduced? However, generations of unwilling Latin scholars had left a rich store of songs, etc., so of course we learned "Amo, amas, I loved a lass," and one which Mother dismissed as silly and ungrammatical but *I* thought funny:

Boyibus kissibus
Sweet Girliorum,
Girlibus likeabus,
Wanty some moreum.

My parents and uncles and aunts were children in the early days of Learning without Tears and they learned all their Latin rules in verse. Unfortunately, I can only remember one and a bit of another. The whole one is:

After verbs to remember, to pity, forget,
The genitive case must be properly set.

And nouns that use "in" instead of "ad" (as in Bethlehem in "Adeste Fideles") include:

> . . . add to these
> Females, cities, countries, trees.

Now that I am old I know another, the *real* reason for Latin besides speaking proper English. It is to understand *mottoes*. Almost all good mottoes are written in Latin and their proper understanding is one of the real blessings of life. The motto of my native city, Belfast, was (and I suppose still is) "Pro Tanto Quid Retribuamus?" Mother said it meant, as in Psalm 116, "What shall I render unto the Lord for all His benefits towards me?" or simply "What shall I do in return for so much?" but Daddy had a story of a Mayor of Belfast who was asked what the city's motto meant and he replied, "What the hell would it mean but No Surrender?"

Other mottoes which I can read because of the Latin of my youth are, besides that of Canada which I learnt much later, "Nec tamen consumebatur" and "Ardens sed verens," both concerned with the Burning Bush; and a riddle of Daddy's, "Animus tuus ego et ignis via," which means "Mind your eye and fire away," and that, of course, is the other use of Latin, to make a secret language for children, pig Latin, or even words like "Cave."

History

Then there was a spot of history known to Daddy and all my uncles (it has no beginning or end so I suppose part is missing):

66

Oh, Rob Roy was a tailor bold, King of the
    Cannibal Islands.
For spoiling a pair of trousers he was banished
    to the Highlands.

You're right me boy, hould up your head and
    look like a gentleman, sir,
And tell me who Napoleon was, now tell me
    if you can, sir.

Napoleon was the King of France before the
    Revolution,
But he got killed at Waterloo which ruined his
    Constitution.

You're right me boy, hould up your head, etc.

Miscellaneous School Traditions

It is a fact, attested to by generations of children, that masters marking examinations stand at the foot of the stairs and throw the papers up, letting them land in whatever order they will.

It is a fact that at boarding schools they paint the butter on the bread with a tiny brush.

It is a fact that a new boy every year goes to have his mouth measured for a spoon.

The following names really describe what school food is made of: fish eyes in glue, dead baby, cat's eyes, etc., etc. (Someone found an identifiable piece of each.)

"Alas, regardless of their doom the little victims play," but listen:

There is a boarding school
Far far away
Where they have onion soup
Three times a day.
Oh how the boarders yell
When they hear the dinner bell!
Oh how the onions smell
Three times a day.

The headmasters with their rods, the oppression of the dead languages, the tyranny of the Rule of Three and mental arithmetic, the legends of dead baby and onion soup... Is all this the present for which we asked every morning and which we have now received?

Pro Tanto Quid Retribuamus?

The Belfast Coat of Arms

6. Salt, Mustard, Cayenne Pepper

When I was young, children had far more free time than they do today. We went to school from nine until noon, once a week we had dancing class, once a week a music lesson, but, for the rest, we were free. We rode our bicycles, we walked, we went for summer holidays at the seaside, we went to parties and to picnics, and we played every day for long hours, in all seasons. We played in the house, on the street, in the schoolyard, at picnics, we played everywhere. As soon as we were old enough we were shoved up, boys first, into *sports*, an adult preoccupation and a way of life. But first we played.

Ring-a-Ring-a-Rosy

All children who speak English, wherever they live, play "Ring Around a Rosy." Each group has its own words, but here is the way children *I* knew played their first game:

Ring-a-ring-a-rosy,
A pocketful of posies.
Asha! Asha!
All fall down.

Toddlers and grown-ups, even an occasional baby in arms, played these first games together. I hear them, not in the piping voices of children, but in the deep voices of uncles and the warm, laughing voices of Mammy and assorted aunts. Another favourite family game of ours on Sunday afternoons was:

> The grand old Duke of York
> He had ten thousand men.
> He marched them up to the top of the hill
> And he marched them down again.
> When they were up they were up,
> When they were down they were down,
> And when they were only halfway up
> They were neither up nor down.

My clearest memory of this is with Paddy, just learning to walk, holding tightly to his father's hand and smiling securely. Partners! I remember Paddy in all these games because he was six years younger than me and I could watch his radiant little face and hear his valiant singing:

> "The child wants a nurse,
> The child wants a nurse,
> Heigho my deary-o,
> The child wants a nurse."

One Follow-the-Leader type of game which was very popular with us I have never heard since. It was played either in a marching ring or in a line:

> I'm a wee Filory Man,
> My father was an Irishman.
> I'll do all that ever I can
> To follow the wee Filory Man.

A new leader moved up each round, and we played until everyone had had a turn. I suppose the first two lines should have been sung by the leader and the rest by his obedient followers. We all sang everything.

As we grew a little older, we took part in family dances on Sunday afternoons. These were very informal and were really an extension of the games. The moving spirit in this was Uncle Toe. He loved dancing, and his nephews and nieces, his sisters and their husbands, joined in the merriment. We did waltzes and polkas, Sir Roger de Coverley, Lancers, and my favourite, "The Velita." I would rush in from Sunday School crying, "Can we do the breezy one, Uncle Toe?"

Music was provided by an old gramophone with a horn, and the little dog listening to his master's voice was on most of the records. We also sang, if we had breath enough, but our range of tunes was small. "The Velita" was done to a record called "Night of Gladness" and polkas to "You Should See Me Dance the Polka":

> You should see my coattails flying
> As I carry my partner round.
> When the band commences playing
> My feet begin to go,
> For a rare old, jolly old polka
> Is the merriest thing I know.

Sometimes for a change we danced the polka to:

> Yip yip yip tooraliaddy.
> And it's yip yip yip tooraliay,
> For there's no better king in the universe
> Than King Edward the Seventh today!

And the babies were taught to polka to "My Aunt Jane She Called Me In."

I loved waltzes too but, for some reason, the only tune I can remember waltzing to is "The Merry Widow," perhaps because we sang to it:

> Though I say not what I may not let you hear,
> Still the swaying dance is saying "Tell me, dear."
> Every touch of fingers seems to let you know —
> Says to you, "'Tis true, 'tis true, I love you so."

We also knew a different set of words, learnt from our American cousins, Hugh and Jeannette Wylie. Mother didn't care for them.

> I wear my pink pyjamas in the summertime,
> I wear my blue pyjamas in the wintertime.
> Sometimes in the springtime and sometimes in
>   the fall
> I go to bed with no pyjamas on at all.

At dancing class (which I also loved) we had a greater variety of both music and dances, but they somehow seemed to be kept separate and did not influence the dancing at home. At dancing class there was much more formality but better and more varied music, also up-to-date music, for the World War I period! We swung our arms and danced to "Chu Chin Chow" and "The Maid of the Mountains":

> Whate'er befall I'll still recall
> That sunlit mountainside
> Where skies are blue and hearts are true
> And love's the only guide.

The next two lines I have forgotten, probably because I didn't understand them, but the ending is clear and happy:

Love holds the key to set me free
And love will find the way.

This conjures up a happy picture of Daddy and Mammy
sitting in the heather on Cave Hill, in sunshine, and Mammy
is wearing her "scrumptious" hat with the blue corded
ribbons and forget-me-nots on it.

At children's parties we played singing games; they were
a feature of the affair like crackers, trifle, fruit salad, and
little sandwiches. Where Canadian children play "London
Bridge Is Falling Down" we played "Here Are the Robbers
Coming Through":

Here are the robbers coming through,
Coming through, coming through,
Here are the robbers coming through,
My fair lady.

What did the robbers do to you,
Do to you, do to you?
What did the robbers do to you,
My fair lady?

Broke my watch and stole my chain,
Stole my chain, stole my chain,
Broke my watch and stole my chain,
My fair lady.

(One is caught and chooses sides.)

Off to prison he must go,
He must go, he must go.
Off to prison he must go,
My fair lady.

(Tug of war at end.)

"Nuts in May" we liked too, although it was one of my first meetings with nepotism. Olive Feeney insisted, "We'll have Mammy Feeney for Nuts in May," or George Iliff demanded that the choice be their little maid Euphemia, "We'll have Feemey Iliff for Nuts in May," and the convention seemed to be that the host family had the right to choose.

Other party games that we played included "Blindman's Buff," "Hunt the Slipper," "Hide the Thimble," "In and Out the Windows," and a ring game called "Paddy from Cork." A ring was borrowed from a grown-up and slipped over a long string which was then held up with both hands by the circle of children. One child stood in the centre while the others passed the ring around, hidden under the covering hands:

> Paddy from Cork has never been,
> Never a railway train has seen,
> Never has seen the great machine
> That runs on the iron railway.

As the song ended, the one in the centre had three guesses as to the whereabouts of the ring. If he found it, the person who had it took his place in the centre. Sad to say this game is no longer played; I suppose it would be called "racist" today for it laughs at the poor ignorant Irishman. We Irish children loved it.

Street Games

I don't know why street games and party games were different and seldom overlapped. There *is* a picture of me aged about two and a half, with my fists up, playing "For We Are Roman Soldiers" in the garden with my big cousins Kitty and Barbara. I remember once playing

"Jinny Jo" at a party, but these were exceptions. For the most part what we thought of as street games were played on the street. One that we all knew was "Roman Soldiers." Remember this was in the days of innocence of the children of Ulster. We hadn't yet seen an armoured car or had an imposed curfew or learned about fear or violence.

(Side One advancing, hands outstretched, palms up)

Will you give us bread and wine,
Bread and wine, bread and wine?
Will you give us bread and wine
For we are Roman soldiers?

(Side Two advancing, hands outstretched, thumbs down)

No, we won't give you bread and wine,
Bread and wine, bread and wine.
No, we won't give you bread and wine
For we are British soldiers.

(Side One advancing, fists up)

Then are you ready for a fight,
For a fight, for a fight?
Then are you ready for a fight
For we are Roman soldiers?

(Side Two advancing, fists up)

Yes, we're ready for a fight,
For a fight, for a fight.
Yes, we're ready for a fight
For we are British soldiers.

(Fight or tug of war)

On the street we played quite regularly a long and very tiresome game called "Jinny Jo." A line of children advances singing the questions which are answered by another child, behind whom Jinny Jo is hiding.

Came to see Jinny Jo, Jinny Jo, Jinny Jo.
Came to see Jinny Jo, is she within?

Jinny Jo's washing clothes, washing clothes,
    washing clothes.
Jinny Jo's washing clothes, can't see her today.

Came to see Jinny Jo, Jinny Jo, Jinny Jo.
Came to see Jinny Jo, is she within?

Jinny Jo's ironing clothes, ironing clothes,
    ironing clothes.
Jinny Jo's ironing clothes, can't see her today.

After that Jinny becomes "Sick in bed, sick in bed, sick in bed," followed by "Jinny Jo's dead and gone, dead and gone, dead and gone." Then the line asks:

What shall we dress her in, dress her in, dress her in?
What shall we dress her in? Shall it be red?

Red is for the soldiers, the soldiers, the soldiers,
Red is for the soldiers so that will not do.

Then we discard blue which is for the sailors, black which is for the mourners, and at last try white:

White is for the dead and gone, dead and gone,
    dead and gone,
White is for the dead and gone so that will just do.

But Jinny Jo, resurrected somehow, comes shrieking after the line, and the one she catches becomes the new Jinny Jo and the whole thing starts again.

Mother had a number of singing games from her youth in the 1880s. They sound much more interesting than ours, but by the time I grew curious about them she was too old and had forgotten them all. Scraps that I remember point to an older, more traditional source. She had a number of beautiful old flower names and recognized many of the flowers in Mary Webb's *Precious Bane*. The only one I can remember is for the purple weed that we call vetch. Mother called it fitchy-pea.

Our game of

> "What's your name?" — Mary Jane.
> "Where do you live?" — Down the lane

I tried on Mother, and she responded with:

> "What's your name?" — Curds and
>   cream.   (*pronounced crame*)
> "What do they call you?" — Pudgy
>   dolly.   (*pronounced dawly*)

Instead of the very dull and ordinary "Jinny Jo," Mother had two similar games that went like this:

> We are three knights, we come from Spain,
> We come to woo your daughter Jane.
> — My daughter Jane is yet too young
> To be controlled by anyone,

and

> Here's an old woman from Sandyland

77

With all her children by the hand.
One can dance and one can sew
And one can make the lilywhite grow.

Another game that Mother knew which we also played
was:

King William was King George's son,
Of the royal race he sprung.
He had a star upon his breast
With points to the East and points to the West.

Down on the carpet you shall kneel
While the grass grows round your feet.
Stand up straight upon your feet
And choose the one you love so sweet.

Now they're married, life and joy,
First a girl and then a boy.
Seven years after, seven years to come,
O Geordie, Geordie, kiss and run.

We always sang "Geordie, Geordie," but Mother knew
either "Fire on the mountain, kiss and run" or "Scotland's
burning, kiss and run."
A round game of Mother's was called "Quaker Meeting."
We found it rather boring because it consists of sitting in a
ring and nodding, Number One starting and the others as
they speak, until the whole ring is nodding:

1. "Neighbour, Neighbour, how art thee?"
2. "Very well, I thank thee."
1. "How is Neighbour next to thee?"
2. "I don't know but I will see."
(Repeat with 2 and 3, 3 and 4, 4 and 5, etc.)

A variant was:

1. "Old Mrs. McQuade's dead."
2. "How did she die?"
1. "She died with her finger up like I."
(Or any other way that the first child likes.)

Counting Out

Mostly we just used "Eeny meeny miny mo" but every few weeks we would try another just for variety for a little while. One we liked was:

One potato, two potatoes, three potatoes, *four*,
Five potatoes, six potatoes, seven potatoes, *more*.
O U T spells OUT and OUT you must go.

We passed this one to Daddy who liked it very much and used it as a chant.

A little English girl called Sybil Hawes taught us:

Piggy on *the* railway
Picking up stones.
Down came *an* engine
And broke Piggy's bones.
"*Oh*," cried Piggy,
"That's not fair."
"Oh," cried *the* engine,
"*I* don't care."

We always said this as we had been taught it, trying to imitate the "fai-ah" and "ca-ah" and also emphasizing all the unimportant words. "This," Sybil explained, "is to be quite fai-ah."

That you could count out *unfairly* had not yet occurred to us but Mother had a verse about cheating which went with jackstones, a game she played very fast and well. It was a most skilful accomplishment with no commercial jacks, just smooth pebbles from the beach and no ball.

> Nancy Ann took it out of the pail
> And she wrapped it up in her petticoat tail,
> And she rolled it in and she rolled it out,
> And if I'd a-been cheatin' I would have been out.

She also taught us to count out to:

> One two three four five,
> I caught a fish alive.
> Six seven eight nine ten,
> I let it go again.
> *Why* did you let it go?
> Because it bit my finger so.

For bouncing ball and skipping we used mostly the same rhymes and we had no great variety:

> Salt — mustard — cayenne pepper —

with the rope or the ball getting faster and faster.

For ball bouncing we nearly always used:

> One two three O'Leary,
> Four five six O'Leary,
> Seven eight nine O'Leary,
> Ten O'Leary Postman.

We skipped to:

> House to let,
> Apply within.
> Jenny jump out
> And Jim jump in,

or:

> Teddy Bear, Teddy Bear, turn around,
> Teddy Bear, Teddy Bear, touch the ground.
> Teddy Bear, Teddy Bear, show your shoe,
> Teddy Bear, Teddy Bear, run right through.

Then there was a completely meaningless one which went:

> Gypsy Gypsy in her tent
> Couldn't afford to pay the rent.
> Policeman came and took all her money,
> Left her nothing but bread and honey.

At the end of a game as the swing died down, or the rope grew slower, or the rocking chair stopped, we chanted this doggerel:

> Die, die, little dog, die,
> Die for the sake of your grandmother's eye.
> A penny to put in the purse,
> A penny to pay the nurse.
> Die, die, little dog, die,
> Die for the sake of your grandmother's eye.

Mother hated this one. She said it was extremely silly, but she confided to me once that in her childhood she said it too.

We probably played these games all year round, but my picture of them now is always in March, with a blue Irish spring sky, full of moving white clouds, a faint but welcome sun, and daffodils in the newly cleaned windows. Then my cup of happiness overflowed and no matter how silly the song, we sang it with joy.

Much too soon for us the adult world closed in. We were bought cricket bats and hockey sticks and we learnt catch words like L B W — meaning "leg *in front of* wicket," or "tackle him low," or "no hitting below the belt." We also joined crowds of cheering children, marching through the streets, waving ribbons and shouting:

>"Methody beat them all!
>Methody beat them all!
>They won two to one,
>Methody on the ball!"

When Daddy heard this one he snorted and cried:

>"Our Queen won!
>Our Queen won!
>Heigho! Bravo!
>Our Queen won!"

Once the boys had moved up and learned cricket and rugby and soccer, they no longer joined in the street games. For a while, girls played cricket in the back garden and hockey at school with the occasional nostalgic game of "Jinny Jo" or "Here Are the Robbers Coming Through," usually with the excuse of helping younger girls, and still younger boys, with the words. There was definitely now a loss of dignity in this kind of play. I think if I had been good at sports I would have welcomed the change, but unlike all the other members of my family (or so I thought)

I was very poor indeed. I tried to keep my eye on the ball, but then, as now, I was unable to judge distance. I could, however, remember the words of the chants and songs and thus, to a small extent, fake the sporting appearance.

I lamented with the referee who cried:

> Oh they tossed me in the air and they rolled me
>   in the mud,
> And then they tried to stop the circulation
>   of my blood,
> And if you live to be as old as me you'll never catch
> Me being the referee at a football match.

Very puzzling was the predicament of the young Welshman who sang:

> My mother told me
> That she would buy me
> A football jersey
> To play for Swansea.
> My mother said if
> I played for Cardiff
> She wouldn't buy me
> A football jersey.

There were football idols too:

> The interval was welcome too —
> We ate ice-cream and Irish stew —
> And Elliman's embrocation too
> At the foot-i-ball match
> Last Saturday.

> When we entered the second half
> The ladies all began to laugh

And said, "Oh my, just look at that calf"
At the foot-i-ball match
Last Saturday.

It was sometimes hard to distinguish between local champions and world-famous sportsmen. To complicate things still further, there were fictional heroes as well. Daddy played football long ago with a youth named Sam Waddell, whose young sister Helen became a distinguished author. I thought all my childhood that this was Sam Weller of the *Pickwick Papers* whose big boot had been placed right in my daddy's face! And my first acquaintance with a sentimental song of the era was in this sporting parody:

After the ball was centred,
After the ball was through,
Barron got up his temper
And away with the ball he flew.
He passed the ball to Gibson,
Gibson had a fall,
And Scott ran out of the goalpost
After the ball!

A particularly furious game would bring forth this:

Then big Black the Loyalists' custodian
Lost more teeth than there are keys in a melodeon —
Off side, on side, one a side and two a side,
At half time we were really playing suicide.

Sports were a real feature of my childhood, and sports honours were jealously treasured (like Uncle Charlie's cricket cap, etc.). We celebrated St. Patrick's Day at the School's Cup Finals shouting for Inst to win over Methody or Campbell, and twisted those curious noisemakers called corncrakes with abandon.

On Saturday afternoons our quiet roads were filled with men, crowds of them, on their way to some sporting event or other. I wonder if others besides me liked the singing better than the play as we chanted:

"Academy beat them all!
Academy beat them all!
We won two to one,
Academy on the ball!"

7. Come Along to the Queen's Arcade

The world of commerce and finance was all around me from the very beginning, I suppose, but I had no understanding of it and was not really aware of its presence. To this day, however, I waken while it is still dark, sometime around four a.m., at that hour when, long ago, the Island whistles blew, and all over Belfast the tramcars started taking the Islandmen to work. On Sunday mornings we climbed up to the top of Cave Hill and looked down at the big ships which the Islandmen were building. We were very proud of the number of great and famous ships that had been built at Harland & Wolff's in Belfast and we knew a song about it although we didn't really understand it (at least I didn't). There was a lot in it about Thor and Odin and Britannia, who seemed to be banging away on an anvil somewhere or hiding in the shadows and spying on one another. It went:

> Clang, clang, clang on the anvil
> In the smithy by the dark North Sea.
> Is it Odin that is watching in the shadows?
> Is it Thor where the sparks fly free?
> Clang, clang, clang on the anvil —
> There are stee-eel shi-ips wanted on the sea.

We knew about the need for ships, they carried cargoes back and forth across the seven seas, and our father taught us a grace:

> For what we are about to eat
> We bless and thank the British fleet.

I was also aware of the linen trade; Irish linen was familiar from my babyhood:

> When I go to bed at night
> I lay my head on linen white.
> Of linen too the snowy sheet,
> Furzy scented, cool and sweet.

I'm not sure where and when I learned this scrap of verse but I was very small when I used to go with Aunt Minnie Whiteford to the linen market in Larne where she would buy sheets and towels and damask tablecloths. If it was a big order and came to an uneven amount like five pounds seventeen and fourpence ha'penny, the small change came to me in the form of a Dutch penny doll or three or four handkerchiefs so fine and soft that five pounds wouldn't buy one of them today. The handkerchiefs and small towels and dresser scarves used to be ironed but the big things like the sheets and damask tablecloths were put through the mangle until they were smooth and shone. Daddy sang:

> "Cheer, boys, cheer,
> Me Mother's got a mangle.
> Cheer, boys, cheer,
> She fills it full of stones.
> Cheer, boys, cheer,
> She turns it with the handle,

Cheer, boys, cheer,
For she mangles all me clothes."

The market towns of County Antrim made a skipping rhyme for me long before I had any idea what a market town was:

Belfast!
Lisburn!
Ballymena! Carrickfergus!
Larne —and—
*Ant*rim!

The first career I ever considered was that of a "Wandell Lady" and I told my astonished family that that was what I had set my heart on and that's what I would be when I grew up. The "Wandell Lady" was a shawly lady with a handcart and a voice like a man's who went through the back alleys of the town crying, "Want delf! Want delf!" And if you could persuade your mother to give you an empty china marmalade jar, she would exchange it for a ha'penny balloon. I could think of no more glorious life; all those balloons for your very own, and to be allowed to shout as loud as you pleased, "Wandell! Wandell!" We all knew a rhyme that said:

If I'd as much money as I could spend
I never would cry "Old chairs to mend."

Why not? we wondered. Wasn't that a lovely outdoor livelihood just like a game?

As I grew older I wanted to keep a wee shop, more particularly a wee sweetie shop, as I imagined "My Aunt Jane's," where I had rows and rows of big glass bottles filled with humbugs and black balls and Everton toffee and cokernut chips, pink and white, and sugared almonds. I saw myself weighing them out carefully and then, like Miss Fisher who sold sweeties to Daddy when he was a little boy, I would add an extra one before I wrapped them up in a wee "poke" of twisted paper. I could hear my father's joyful cry, "Hang expense, give the girl a ha'pporth of toffee," and I would get rich.

Rich and Poor

Rich, from all I heard and read, was very desirable although I was never quite sure what it meant or how you got that way. The whole world was divided into the Rich and the Poor and some people had a lot of money and others had nothing at all. It was very puzzling and the answer depended on which grown-up you asked. Were the good rich? Were the poor lazy and shiftless? We learned a children's hymn that made Daddy very angry. It was called "Day by Day the Little Daisy" and it sang the virtues of quiet humility:

> God hath given each his station:
> Some have riches and high place,
> Some have lowly homes and labour,
> All may have God's precious grace.

This annoyed Daddy so much that we stopped going to Sunday School and stayed at home and danced to the gramophone with Uncle Toe, but the riddle of the rich and poor remained unsolved. Mother sang us a song about it which went like this:

> I'll sing you a good old song made by a good
> old pate

Of a fine old Irish gentleman who owned an
old estate
And who kept up his old mansion at a bountiful
old rate
With a good old porter to relieve the old poor
at his gate.

And that, coupled with the Christmas carol of "Good King Wenceslas," taught us that it was blessed to help the poor.

Then there were beggars: children in the street crying, "Gie us a penny, gie us a penny," adults crowding around as you came out of the pictures and asking for your chocolates or sixpences, and *real* beggars with children clinging to their skirts who came to the door every Thursday (why Thursday I don't know), and they got bacon sandwiches and sixpence. They were quiet and well-behaved, unlike the song that said:

Hark, hark, the dogs do bark,
The beggars are coming to town,
Some in rags and some in tags
And some in a velvet gown.

But if you weren't a beggar and you had a father who loved you, the world of business made all sorts of claims upon you and called for your attention. For instance:

Daddy's gone to London where
The streets are paved with gold.
Daddy's gone to London where
The poor are never cold,
Where there's lots of toys
For girls and boys,
And as for Baby Jack
He shall have a Gee-Gee
When our Dad comes back.

Or nearer home:

> Come along to the Queen's Arcade,
> The source of childhood joys,
> Where you can get a dolly or a toy
> For your good little girls and boys.

Money

Money, mysterious as it was, and useful for buying dolls and toys and cokernut chips, seemed to have a main purpose apart from any of these. The Chief End of Money seemed to be Savings, but no one ever confided in us children what the Savings were for. At Aunt Minnie Whiteford's in Larne there was a little stool made of wood and leather with a hole in the top and a pattern in brass nails. These nails read:

> Our wee Whiteford is no fool,
> He puts his pennies in his stool.

It seemed pretty silly to me but Whiteford was no longer wee, he was a man, and presumably he had grown up wise and maybe rich.

A maxim which was often given to guide us was "Take care of the pennies and the pounds will take care of themselves," and we knew a song that assured us if we would:

> Save up all your money
> You'll never be on the rocks,
> And you'll always have tobacco
> In your old tobacco box!

All was not peaceful between the rich and the poor, between the rich men who owned the shops and the factories and the mines and the poor men who worked in them. Sometimes the workers would declare "a Strike" and this made everyone very miserable and the strikers' children were hungry. We saw their pictures in the papers. The first strike I ever knew of was in Dublin where a group of men with placards barred the door to the Maypole Margarine shop crying, "Don't let your daughters work in the English sweatshops." As we hurried past I asked, "Mammy, what is a sweatshop?" but she answered, "Come along, dear, lift your feet." If I had asked an uncle, any uncle, he would have told me, but I never did and I still don't really know what a sweatshop is.

The greatest musical experience of my father's life, he often told us, was on the docks at Barry when a big group of Welsh longshoremen greeted the end of a coal strike by lifting their voices to sing:

"When the coal comes from the Rhonda,
When the coal comes from the Rhonda,
When the coal comes from the Rhonda,
When the coal comes from the Rhonda I'll be there.
With my little pick and shovel I'll be standing on
    the quay;
When the coal comes from the Rhonda I'll be there."

One afternoon Mammy and I went to visit Aunt Jennie and on our way home we waited and waited for a tram but none came. Then someone who was passing said "The strike's on," and soon a band of marching men came through the street singing:

We'll work no more
Till we get the forty-four
On the good ship Yacky Hicky Doola.

"What's the forty-four, Mammy?"
"They only want to work forty-four hours a week."
"Oh, I see."
Then there was a funny song of which we only knew scraps about (a) a wife and (b) a barber who refused to work more than an eight-hour day:

Little Tommy Hooligan
He came home full again.
He knocked at the door, he did,
He shouted through the floor, he did,
"Bridget, let me in."

Bridget heard the shindy
And she opened up the windy.
She looked down below, she did,
She stayed up above, she did.
"I will not let you in.

"For I've worked eight hours this day,
Don't you think I've earned my pay?
You can stay out there
In the rain and swear
For I won't work half a minute longer."

And the barber replied to an irate customer the same way:

"Keep your other whisker on
Till the morning, John,
For I won't work half a minute longer."

All this, of course, led to legislation and labour laws. Of these we heard most about the ones which affected sailors, their food, their space, their working hours, and their holidays. One song we knew was:

Then shout, boys, hurray,
For you know you get your whack.
You get your pound, you get your pint
According to the Act.
And what's the use of grumbling
For you know it must be done
When you are bound in a lime juice ship
On a voyage around the sun.

But were they grateful? Not a bit. Daddy recited:

"Lloyd George no doubt when his life pegs out
Will ride in a fiery chariot,
Seated in state on a red-hot plate
Twixt Satan and Judas Iscariot.
Ananias that day to the Devil will say,
'My claim for precedence now fails.
Move me up one higher, away from the fire,
And make room for the liar from Wales.'"

Advertisements

I was a child in the days of the really great billboards. One of them which the adults found funny moved me to tears. It showed a steer mournfully contemplating a tiny jar of beef extract as he cried, "Alas, my poor brother!" More cheerful was the shipwrecked gentleman in the striped pyjamas who assured us that "Bovril prevents that sinking feeling" as he straddled a bottle of it in the waves. I knew, for the billboards told me, that Glaxo builds bonny babies, and I was familiar with Pears Soap Bubbles and the Gentleman of the Road penning his famous letter: "Some years ago I used your soap. Since then I have used no other." Mother sang us a number of the rhymed advertisements of which I remember:

— They come as a boon and a blessing to men,
  The Pickwick, the Owl, and the Waverley Pen.

— Full many a gem of purest Razorene   (a hair cream)
  The dark unfathomed caves of ocean bear.

— Hark the herald angels sing
  Beecham's pills are just the thing —
  Safe in use, in action mild,
  Two for man and one for child.

There were catch riddles too, like:

— "Can you tell a donkey from a lemon?"
  "No? Well, I won't send you for a dozen lemons."

— "How do you pronounce C-A-S-T-O-R-I-A?"
  "Do you? Doctors pronounce it harmless."

— "Mammy, why does Daddy call that man One and
    Six?"
  "Because his name is Bob Tanner."

On Saturdays I did my part for the world of commerce. I did messages for Mammy and Aunt Kathleen and I was given a penny to spend on myself. I was a careful and patient messenger because I remembered a horrible example:

I gave McCann me can
To fetch a pint of stout.
McCann came running in to say
Me can was running out.
McCann knew me can was new,
I'd only had it a day or two.
I'll put a hole in McCann
For putting a hole in me can.

Most of the commercial riddles of my childhood are still unsolved. Strikes go on and the rich and the poor are still with us. One thing alone has changed. No one seems to save money any more.

8. I Know My Love

Apple jelly, jam tart,
Tell me the name of your sweetheart.

George Orwell, in an essay on the English comic postcard,
says that its humour depends on the very healthy state of
English family life. Old Dad, disporting himself on the
beach at Brighton with a strange blonde, is funny only
because it's ridiculous. That's not what Dad does at all.

In the Ulster of my childhood, marriages were loving
and faithful. We knew no divorced or quarrelling couples
and all our storybooks assured us that "they married and
lived happily ever after." It is strange in the face of all this
that in rhyme and song, husbands and wives should be so
different. Maybe the songs are like the comic postcards,
funny because the reality was different.

Courtship was romantic enough, and, we gathered, full
of pain:

Oh have you been in love, me boys, and have you felt
    the pain?
I'd sooner be in gaol itself than be in love again.
The girl I loved was beautiful, I'd have you
    for to know,
And I met her in the garden where the murphies grow.

This, yards of it, we heard from Daddy, and when I was young I heard "murphies," no matter who sang it.

The pain of love was less rollicking and much more poignant from Mother. She sang:

> "I know where I'm goin'
> And I know who's goin' wi' me.
> I know whom I love
> But the dear knows who I'll marry.
>
> Some say he's black,
> I say he's bonny,
> The fairest of the fair,
> My handsome, coaxin' Johnny."

On the street, and at home as well, we knew another song like this, less plaintive and more practical:

> I'm goin' down the town,
> I know who's goin' wi' me.
> I got a wee boy of my own
> And they call him Dandy Jimmy.
>
> He wears a nice blue coat
> And his waistcoat's in the fashion,
> But he has to lie in bed
> While his Sunday shirt's a-washing.

Mother was an authority on love. She knew about meeting and parting and she had a bonnet trimmed with blue ribbons and little forget-me-nots that I believed to be the subject of many songs like this one:

> I've got a bonnet trimmed with blue.
> "Why don't you wear it?" So I do.

When I go out to see my John
Why then I put my bonnet on.

So well this song seemed to suit my Mammy that I was very puzzled by the lover's name being John. My Daddy's name was Hugh, and if it was rhyme that was needed, why Hugh rhymed with blue.

Another of Mother's sad love songs was:

I know my love by his way of walking,
I know my love by his way of talking.
I know my love by his eyes of blue,
And if my love leaves me, what shall I do?

Her love leave her? Daddy go away? Never! Except to go away to sea and *that* we were looking after in our nightly prayers. Mind you, he certainly didn't seem to take the matter very seriously. One of *his* love songs went:

She's a fine big lump of an Irish a-gir-a-cultural girl.
She neither paints nor powders and her figure is all
    her own,
And she kicks that hard you'd think you was kicked
    by the leg of a mule.
The full of me arms of Irish love is pretty Kitty Sloan.

Whoever this was it was not our mother. Maybe someone called "an old flame." Daddy's song of parting, while it was sad enough and about an Alice at that, turned out to be about two elephants in Barnum and Bailey's circus!

Jumbo said to Alice, "I love you!"
Alice said to Jumbo, "I don't believe you do,
For if you really loved me as you say you do
You wouldn't go to Yankeeland and leave me
    in the zoo."

Even if Jumbo was an elephant he was an unfeeling mon-
ster. Sad, too, was the nursery story of Charlie Chuck:

> Charlie Chuck
> Married a duck.
> The duck died
> And Charlie cried
> Sitting by the fireside.

I really felt that Daddy took a very frivolous view of the
fate of all these unhappy lovers, and when I heard another
of his songs I had grave doubts about his better feelings.
Who would celebrate the beauties of his beloved thus?

> O Katy Connor, I dote upon her.
> Her big feet take up the street
> And stop the tramway cars.
> If she should take the notion
> To dive into the ocean
> I'd never marry Katy
> Till there's whiskers on cigars.

And then there was the fickle wench that poor Tom courted:

> Young Tom he was a farmer's son and he lived
>   way down in Devon,
> And every morn he fed the pigs from half past six
>   to seven.
> For many pretty girls he had a light and fickle fancy
> But oh the one he really loved was sweet young
>   mistress Nancy.

Refrain:

> Oh sing ho sing hey for a merry merry merry maid,
> Her eyes are bright and glowing,

Her eyes are bright and glowing
But what her way with a man will be
My goodness, my goodness, there's no knowing.

Her cheeks were like the apple bloom, her lips were
    like the cherry
And every time she looked at Tom his heart grew
    light and merry,
But oh she was a sad coquette, she quite deserved
    to lose him
For one day she'd accept his suit, the next day
    she'd refuse him.

Young Tom he wooed her for a year but she proved
    proud and haughty
So in despair at last he wed a rich young widow
    of forty.
Now still for pretty girls he has a light and fickle fancy
But none will ever be to him as dear as was sweet Nancy.

Sing ho sing hey for a merry merry merry maid,
Their ways are quaint and funny.
Their ways are quaint and funny.
If you can't find one to marry for love,
My goodness, my goodness, go marry one for
    her money.

Both Daddy and Mammy sang:

"Just jump over the garden wall,
Dear little girlie to me.
I've been lonely a long long time
And the wall's not hard to climb —
You just jump up and you just jump down,
I'll not let you fall.

We'll play at sweethearts going to be married,
Come over the garden wall."

And Mother sang one song with a happy ending:

"Will you accept of the keys of my chest,
Plenty of money at my behest?
Madam, will you walk? Madam, will you talk?
Madam, will you walk and talk with me?

No, I'll not accept of the keys of your chest,
Plenty of money at thy behest,
And I will not walk, and I will not talk,
And I will not walk or talk with you.

Will you accept of a coach and six,
Six little nigger boys black as pitch?
Madam, will you walk? Madam, will you talk?
Madam, will you walk and talk with me?

I'll not accept of your coach and six,
Six little nigger boys black as pitch,
And I will not walk, and I will not talk,
And I will not walk or talk with you.

Will you accept of the keys of my heart,
Only yours until death do us part?
Madam, will you walk? Madam, will you talk?
Madam, will you walk and talk with me?

Yes, I'll accept of the keys of your heart
Only mine until death do us part.
Yes, sir, I will walk, yes, sir, I will talk,
Yes, sir, I will walk and talk with you."

After all these smiles and tears and fairings and so on should come the happy haven of marriage. Sometimes gentlemen were curiously reluctant, as in the case of "Impudent Barney O'Hea":

> Impudent Barney, none of your blarney,
> Impudent Barney O'Hea.
> Impudent Barney, none of your blarney,
> Makes a girl Mistress O'Hea.
>
> So let you begone for I know you won't,
> For I know you won't, for I know you won't.
> Let you begone for I know you won't
> Make a girl Mistress O'Hea.

Even if the young man was eager and willing, sometimes he didn't have the necessary money as in the case of Joe (who got it):

> Darling Mabel, now I'm able
> To buy the happy home.
> Since they've raised my screw, love,
> I've enough for two, love.
> Say you'll marry, do not tarry,
> Answer yes or no.
> I conclude with love and kisses,
> Yours forever, Joe.

So they got married, and if in real life they lived happily ever after, in song they certainly did not. Take the young lover returning from the fair, for instance:

> He promised he'd buy me a basket of posies,
> A garland of lilies, a wreath of red rosies;
> He promised he'd buy me a bunch of blue ribbons
> To tie up my bonny brown hair.

And then take the truculent and miserly husband:

"Jack, sell your fiddle and buy your wife a gown."
"I wouldn't sell my fiddle for all the wives in town."

And the light-hearted way this husband looked at his loss:

On Saturday night I lost my wife,
On Sunday morning I found her —
Up in the moon playing a tune
With all the stars around her.

Or this more modern one:

O Dorothy, Dorothy Dean!
O Dorothy, where have you been?
She's suddenly flown to regions unknown
Along with a man on a flying machine.

Mothers-in-law were a problem too. Listen to this:

You take the hatchet and I'll take the saw
And we'll chop off the head of my mother-in-law.

And mothers-in-law-to-be were very watchful and sus-
picious, like this one:

"I hear someone whistling around the house,
   I'm sure."
"Och, Mother, it's just the wind a-whistling through
   the door."
"I've lived a long time, Mary, in this great world,
   my dear,
But the wind to whistle like that I never before
   did hear."

"And Mother there's the pig onaisy in his mind,
And sure they say you know that pigs can see
    the wind."
"That's all very well in the day, but let me here remark
That a pig no more nor me can see anything in the dark."

So boys, too near the house don't courting go if
    you mind,
Unless you are sartin and sure the old woman's
    both deaf and blind.

In song, at least, marriage is disillusioning. It results in
loss of freedom, money, and peace. But both husbands and
wives in song repeat the mistake again and again:

Again and again and again,
Again and again and again,
Oh when I was single my pockets did jingle
And I long to be single again.

My wife she died, ah then,
My wife she died, ah then,
My wife she died and I laughed till I cried
For now I was single again.

I married another, ah then,
I married another, ah then,
I married another far worse than the other
And I long to be single again.

And then there was the plight of the old farmer who
wished his wife in hell:

There was an old farmer in Yorkshire did dwell,
With a taidy taidy titty fol lol,
And he had an old wife and he wished her in hell,

With a taidy taidy titty fol lol,
With a taidy titty fol lol.

The devil came to him one day at the plough,
Taidy taidy titty fol lol
And told him "Old man, I am taking her now,"
With a taidy taidy titty fol lol,
Taidy titty fol lol.

They were seven years going and nine coming back,
Taidy taidy titty fol lol,
And she asked for the porridge she'd left on the rack,
Taidy taidy titty fol lol,
Taidy titty fol lol.

And that's why the women is worse nor the men,
Taidy taidy titty fol lol,
And that's why the women is worse nor the men,
Taidy taidy titty fol lol,
Taidy titty fol lol.

A more realistic note sounds when the children come along — that keeps the couple so busy that things like jangling pockets and new gowns are forgotten. The song warns:

And then look out for squalls
For when Baby comes, you see,
It will take the both of you most of your time
To look after Number Three.

On a more cheerful note there was one of Daddy's which I loved:

Don't whistle so loud, you naden't be so proud.
Many a boy is a father today
And there might have been two of them,
    Micky O'Dowd.

9. Simple Right and Wrong

Like the worthy young man in Shaw's *Major Barbara*, the Ulster child of my generation knew the difference between simple right and wrong. The Christian graces might be a bit mysterious since they varied from grown-up to grown-up. Uncle Harry laid great stress on closing doors; Mammy on putting toys away and lifting one's feet; Aunt Mollie had some incomprehensible ones (but then she lived in England). All grown-ups agreed on one point: well-behaved children did not whine.

The virtues, however, were another matter. A good child was obedient, truthful, and clean, and since the punishment for breaking these simple rules was swift, sure, and painful, we seldom broke them. "Spare the rod and spoil the child" was a proverb known to us all.

The whole system was presided over by God, a Being so mysterious that even the oldest and wisest of our uncles seemed very ill-informed as to His nature. In fact, my small cousin Paddy remarked admiringly, "God's pretty fly. No one seems to know much about him." However, a great variety of songs, hymns, and proverbs attested to His tastes and attributes. We prayed to Him every night to bring Daddy safely home, to give us our "piece," and to clothe us:

Through each perplexing path of life
Our wandering footsteps guide;
Give us each day our daily bread
And raiment fit provide.

The question that puzzled us here was "If God knows everything as they say He does, why do we have to remind Him to get the right size?"

He also, we gathered, sat day and night watching our doings:

Behold he that keeps Israel
He slumbers not nor sleeps.

And:

For we know the Lord of Glory
Always sees what children do
And is writing now the story
Of our thoughts and actions too.

And:

God is always near me
Hearing what I say,
Knowing all my thoughts and deeds,
All my work and play.

What does God like as He looks upon children at school and at play? The answers are clear and explicit:

Clean hands and clean faces and neatly combed hair
And garments made decent and plain
Are better than all the fine things that we wear
That make us look vulgar and vain.

And: "Tomorrow will be Friday; keep your nose tidy."

(This latter seems to have been the sum total of my learning on my first day at Sunday School. I remember the day very well but no other wisdom except this.)

Apart from cleanliness, God is very particular about not being quarrelsome. On this point God and *all* grown-ups seem to agree:

> Birds in their little nests agree
> And 'tis a shameful sight
> When children of one family
> Fall out and squall and fight.

Or, as my little brother sang Cecil Frances Alexander's hymn:

> "We are but little children weak
> Nor born in any angry state."

God also likes us to be brave and take brave stands, even fight wars on His behalf:

> *Dare* to be a Daniel,
> *Dare* to stand alone,
> *Dare* to have a purpose firm,
> And *dare* to make it known.

Then there was one where we chose sides:

> Who is on the Lord's side? Who will serve the King?
> Who will be His helpers other lives to bring?
> Who will leave the world's side? Who will face the foe?
> Who is on the Lord's side? Who for Him will go?

And another, quite incomprehensible, but very grand:

> Trust no lovely forms of passion,
> Fiends may look like angels bright,
> But in every word and action
> Trust in God and do the right.
> Trust no party, sect, or faction,
> Trust no leaders in the fight, etc. etc.

We were urged to avoid the Devil and all His works: "Tell the truth and shame the Devil," and:

> Some say the Divil's dead,
> Some say he's hardly,
> Some say the Divil's dead
> And buried in Killarney.

> Some say he'll rise again,
> Rise again, rise again,
> Some say he'll rise again
> And dance the Hieland Laddie.

(He was really buried in Kirkaldy, but we always had him in Killarney.)

Then, of course, the catechism requires us to keep the Sabbath Day. The fourth commandment is long but, we gathered, God sets great store by it:

> Remember the Sabbath-Day to keep it holy. Six days shalt thou labour and do all thy work; but the seventh day is the Sabbath of the Lord thy God: in it thou shalt not do any work, thou, nor thy son, nor thy daughter, thy man-servant nor thy maid-servant, nor thy cattle, nor thy stranger that is within thy gates: for in six days the Lord made Heaven and earth, the

sea and all that in them is, and rested the seventh day:
wherefore the Lord blessed the Sabbath Day and
hallowed it.

When Mammy was a little girl she learned:

This is Sunday, Sabbath Day,
That is why you mustn't play,
Run about or make a noise
Like the naughty girls and boys.

Even getting *born* on Sunday makes for a perfect child:

Monday's child is fair of face,
Tuesday's child is full of grace,
Wednesday's child is full of woe,
Thursday's child has far to go,
Friday's child is loving and giving,
Saturday's child works hard for a living,
But the child that is born on the Sabbath Day
Is blithe and bonny and good and gay.

This was all perfectly clear but the grown-up inter-
pretation of it was not. In fact, of all grown-up incon-
sistencies, this was the greatest. I am reported to have run
to Mammy with the information, "Daddy's singing, and
they're not Sunday songs either." Uncle Toe danced with
us on Sundays; other uncles played cricket (of which the
neighbours disapproved). Quite evidently a foolish con-
sistency was not a grown-up failing!

The rewards of this system and the punishments were
too remote to concern us greatly. It is true that the wicked
go to Hell when they die but children aren't wicked,
they're naughty, and anyway death is a whole lifetime
away. Hell, then, becomes a word to say when the grown-

ups are not listening, or when, for some reason, it is all right. Daddy's friend Captain Milner taught us a lovely song that went:

> Oh, Jenny Brown she baked my bread
> And you bet she baked it well.
> She baked it hard as anything,
> She baked it hard as . . . Hallelujah!
> Keep your seats for I'm not swearing . . . Hallelujah!
> And the truth I always tell.

There was an American one which Daddy and Mammy and the uncles sang but where it came from I don't know:

> Way down yonder in Yankety Yank
> A bullfrog jumped from bank to bank
> 'Cos he hadn't nothing else to do.
> He stubbed his toe and in he fell
> And the neighbours say he went to. . . We. .ell
> 'Cos he hadn't nothing else to do.

> Now, jes' lots of folks are like this foolish frog o' mine,
> A-running into trouble jes' to pass the time,
> And the Devil's always lopin' round here jes' to catch
>   the kind
> That never haven't nothin' else to do.

> When they buried that frog Preacher said:
> "Reason why this frog am dead,
> He never hadn't nothin' else to do.
> So all you folks better listen to me,
> You better stay at home with your fambily
> When you haven't nothin' else to do."

> 'Cos jes' lots of folks are like this foolish frog o' mine
> A-running into trouble jes' to pass the time

And the Devil's always lopin' round here, jes' to catch
      the kind
That never haven't nothin' else to do.

Heaven was, fortunately, equally remote. My small cousin
Betty had a hymn that seemed to keep her safe:

Little children will be there
What has long and curly hair,
What has sought the Lord by prayer
In every Sabbath School.

Betty's hair was short and straight and prayer was not one
of her activities; she found her hymn very comforting.

Another song or rather hymn which is, I realize now,
about Heaven, I always thought was a celebration of the
joys of a nearby park called The Waterworks. It had two
ponds, reservoirs, I suppose, and green banks leading down
to them. Here I went and fed the swans or ran breathless
down the banks holding the hands of two grown-ups,
Mammy and Daddy or Mammy and "one of the uncles."
The verse I liked best seemed to me to take place in the
hall at 83 Cedar Avenue where two of us waited impatiently
for Mother:

Come to that happy land,
Come, come away.
Why will you doubting stand?
Why still delay?
        . . . . .
On then to glory run,
Be a crown and kingdom won,
And bright above the sun
Reign, reign for aye.

(I didn't understand why it rained above the sun.)

A great variety of moral precepts accompanied this basic code of good and evil. These ranged all the way from copy-book maxims to riddles and music-hall rules of conduct. Here is a selection:

— Whatever you do, do with your might
For things done by halves are never done right.

— Some things are better left unsaid;
Carefully consider this before you go ahead.
Sometimes a gentle hint is best:
Drop a hint and let imagination do the rest.

— A stitch in time saves nine.

— A bad workman quarrels with his tools.

— It's not the hen that cackles the most that lays
the largest egg.

— A place for everything and everything in its place.

And from Daddy:

— Keep your eyes and your ears open and your mouth shut.

— Obey on the double; question afterwards.

— Children that eat sweeties before dinner are as bad as secret drinkers.
(This suggested really furtive vice.)

— Some books are lies frae end tae end
And some great lies were never penned.

E'en meenisters they hae been kenned
   In holy rapture
A rousin' quid at times tae send
   Anailt wi' scripture.

Bible Riddles

These were acquired at home. I don't think I learned any of them on the street although many other riddles came from contemporaries. Besides the one mentioned earlier about "The Son of Pharoah's Daughter" we loved Samson's riddle for it appeared on the green and gold tins of Lyle's Golden Syrup, a World War I sugar substitute. There was the dead lion covered with bees, unappetizing to the grown-ups but beautiful to us children. "Out of the strong cometh forth sweetness."

Then we knew:

— Why can you never be hungry in a desert? — Because of the sand which is there.

— Why are there sandwiches there? — Because Ham mustered and bred there.

— Palm Sunday? — Oh, yes, the day when all good Christians go to church with crowns on their heads and palms on their hands.

— Why did Eve never get the measles? — She 'ad Adam.

— Who was the first man in the Bible? — Chap One.

— Who was the shortest man in the Bible? — Bildad the Shuhite.

115

And pointless to the child in 1982 and almost equally so to the child of 1914:

— Methusaleh was the oldest man who ever lived but he died before his father.
— Enoch never saw death; he was translated.

Lastly, of course, the one *everyone* knows:

— Where was Moses when the light went out?

Another moral code quite different from that of the grown-ups and God, but far more influential, was the peer-group standard of worth. As God and parents hated quarrelling and whining, children hated tale-telling, butting in out of turn, keeping things like sweeties to oneself, and general unfairness.

Tell tale tit
Your tongue shall be slit
And every doggy in the town
Will get a little bit.

Precepts passed down from child to child were:

— Finders keepers,
Losers weepers.

— Turnabout is fair play.

— First come, first served (but grown-ups in stores did not obey).

— Ladies first except when taking medicine (my brave little brother).

— Ladies first except on ladders (I didn't understand this one).

— The one who divides the apple must let the other choose his share.

— The owner of a bag of sweets must pass it. He can spread it out on the footpath and divide it openly but he cannot take first choice. Also he must not wince when the one he wanted goes.

But at the family table one may claim one's own: "It's my turn for the heel, he had it yesterday!"

In spite of all that the grown-ups say (and Sunday School), Tit for Tat is fair.

One last street one which I didn't understand because it is part of the adult code but is yelled by children:

Stick your head in the porridge pot
And don't call me "What?"

A great gulf between the generations lies in the fact that children are convinced that all grown-ups want model children. Children *hate* them. Witness this model of virtuous childhood:

"I love you, Mother," said little John.
Then, forgetting his word, his cap was on
And he was off to the garden swing
And left her wood and water to bring.

"I love you, Mother," said little Nell,
"I love you more than tongue can tell."
(Then she teased and pouted half the day

Till Mother rejoiced when she went to play.)
(I had forgotten this part.)

"I love you, Mother," said little Fan.
"Today I'll help you all I can.
How glad I am school doesn't keep,"
And she rocked the baby fast asleep.

Then stepping softly she brought her broom
And swept the floor and tidied the room.
Busy and happy all day was she,
Healthy and happy as child can be.

"We love you, Mother," they all of them said,
Three little children going to bed.
How do you think their mother guessed
Which of them really loved her best?

Such virtue called forth our scorn:

Teacher's Pet . . . yah, yah!
Mammy's Boy . . . yah, yah!
Goody good . . . yah, yah!

We much preferred:

— "Pudding and pie,"
Said Jane. "Oh, my!"
"Which would you rather?"
Said her father.
"*Both*," said Jane
Quite bold and plain.

— "Enfant gâte, veux-tu du pâté?"
"Non, Maman, il est trop salé."

"Veux-tu du rôti?"
"Non, Maman, il est trop cuit."

— Little Polly Flinders
Sat among the cinders
Warming her pretty little toes.
Her mother came and caught her
And whipped her little daughter
For spoiling her nice new clothes.

— A diller, a dollar, a ten o'clock scholar,
What makes you come so soon?
You used to come at ten o'clock
But now you come at noon.

— "Go to bed," says Sleepyhead.
"Sit up a while," says Slow.
"Put on the pot," says Greedy Sot,
"We'll eat before we go."

These were children we knew and understood.

The mountains of Mourne, County Down

Donegall Place, Belfast

10. The Hand on the Funnel

My father used to tell us that the second most beautiful sight in the world was Sydney Harbour at sunset. "But what's the *most* beautiful, Daddy?" we would ask. "Oh, Belfast Lough on a June morning," he replied, as if everyone knew *that*.

It was the only city we had seen and while it was not very large or imposing, and inclined to be grey and wet, it was ringed around with hills and the sea came up to its doors, bringing ships from far away. Great ships were built there too at Harland and Wolff's on The Island. Our lives were touched everywhere by the sea. Most of our friends, and four of our cousins, were seamen's children: the Iliffs, the Moores, the Hannas, and others. Some of them grew up and took to the sea in their turn. Of others it was regretfully reported that they had swallowed the anchor.

In school every morning we took it in turn to choose the opening hymn. My choice varied with a fickle taste but George Iliff always chose the same:

> Star of Peace to wanderers weary,
> Bright the beam that smiles on me,
> Cheer the pilot's vision dreary
> Far, far at sea.
> Cheer the pilot's vision dreary
> Far, far at sea.

"Nonsense," was Daddy's reaction to this, but still we sang it. Mother had another, not a hymn, but we felt it was much the same:

> White wings they never grow weary,
> They carry me cheerily over the sea.
> Night comes, I long for my dearie,
> I'll spread out my white wings and sail home to thee.

The attitude in both of these was the same as our nightly prayers which kept begging God to bring Daddy home. Does the sailor really want to come home from the sea? Even as a child I sometimes wondered.

Daddy's own songs were quite different. They were songs of the sea: work songs, sagas, funny songs. Daddy would storm through the house of a morning calling or chanting:

> "Rise and shine on the Black Ball Line!
> Show a leg for a sea-boot!"

and we were expected to stick legs out from under the blankets to show we were awake. (It worked best with small visiting cousins!)

My father had no ear and always (like me) sang off-key, but he had a well-developed rhythmic sense which the chanteys reinforced. They were work songs with a purpose, to keep the crew together as they raised sails or performed other duties:

> Oh, the anchor is weighed and the sails they are set,
>   Way — Rio,
> And the maids that we're leaving we'll never forget,
> For we're bound for the Rio Grande,
>   And away — Rio,

> Haul away — Rio,
> And it's fare thee well, my bonny wee girl,
> For we're bound for the Rio Grande.
>
> So pack up your donkey and get underway,
> Way — Rio,
> And the girls that we're leaving can take our half pay
> For we're bound for the Rio Grande.

Sunday mornings, especially in summer, brought:

> In Mobile Bay where I was born,
> Mark well what I do say,
> I used to work each sunny morn,
> Oh, roll the cotton down!

or:

> Hey for Reuben Ranzo!
> Ranzo, boys, Ranzo!

Many words were sung to the tune I know as "God Save Ireland." As a child I knew five or six, but it wasn't until I came to Canada that I learned:

> Beneath the Union Jack
> We will wave the Fenians back.

Daddy sang — and worked to:

> 'Bout ship's stations, lads, be handy,
> Raise tack, sheet, and mainsail haul.
> O Johnny come back, haul in the slack,
> Round away the capstan, heave a pawl — heave a pawl.

But he also taught us:

> "God save Ireland!" cried the prisoner;
> "God save Ireland" say we all.
> Whether on the gallows high
> Or on battlefield we die,
> 'Tis no matter if for Ireland we fall.

The first line may be prisoner, hero, soldier, patriot, as your fancy takes you.

There was a sad one too which we didn't understand but had our suspicions about:

> O Tommy's gone and I'm goin' too,
> Tom's gone to Hilo.

One reason for the sadness of this song was that it was nearly always followed by a scrap of verse, without music, which went:

> And oh dear friends 'tis I would be
> Out there with you beneath the sea
> Sleeping sound, sleeping sound like gentlemen.

One chantey which seemed to have been written especially for Daddy was:

> Oh we'll rant and we'll roar like true British seamen,
> We'll rant and we'll roar across the salt seas
> Until we strike soundings in the Channel of Old
>   England —
> From Ushant to Scillies is tharty-five leagues.
>
> Farewell and adieu to you then, Spanish ladies,

> Farewell and adieu to you ladies ashore,
> For we've received orders to sail to the Southward
> And you charming ladies will see us no more.

That could be heard at any time of the day or night and seemed to suit any occasion or mood.

"A Sailor's Alphabet" I knew from my very early days and I think Mammy taught me more of it than Daddy. It was a very long time ago, before we left Cedar Avenue, and I have forgotten most of it because I was too small to understand it. If I heard the verses again I'm sure I would remember them.

> A is the Anchor of our jolly boat,
> B is the . . .that sets her afloat,
>
> So merry, so merry, so merry are we,
> There's none like a sailor that sails on the sea.
> Blow high, blow lo-ow as the ship glides along,
> Give a sailor his grog and there'll nothing go wrong.

There was one which, we realized, was altered from time to time, and some of the words applied to particular people and places. These words, which we sang the same way over and over again, are, I think, from a book of sea chanteys which was in the house and which I read. I think the words are not my memory of an oral but a visual experience.

> A Yankee ship came down East River,
>   Blow, boys, blow.
> Her masts did bend, her sails did shiver,
>   Blow, boys, bully boys, blow.
>
> Her sails were old, her sides were rotten,
> His charts the skipper had forgotten.

Who d'ye think was skipper of her?
Old Preaching Sam the noted scoffer.

Her mate was Joe the Frisco digger,
Her bo'sun was a great black nigger.

Her "chips" was not a proper sailor,
Her "sails" was just a jobbing tailor.

And what d'ye think they had for dinner?
'Twas water soup but slightly thinner.

This ship set out for London City
But never got there, more's the pity.

"Shenandoah" (pronounced Shenandore) was my great
favourite and moved me to tears although I never knew why:

O Sally Brown, I love your daughter,
Away you rolling river. . .

Was it a girl or was it a river that he loved, and why did he
love her so? Other girls in other songs were soon forgotten
or better left behind:

Oh once I loved an Irish girl but she was fat and lazy,
Oh away, haul away, come haul away together,
Haul away Joe!

Oh once I loved an American girl but she was fond
    of whiskey,
Oh away, haul away, come haul away together,
Haul away Joe!

And speaking of whiskey there was a rollicking one about it:

> Whiskey is the life of man,
>   Whiskey Johnny!
> Whiskey in an old tin can,
>   Whiskey for my Johnny.
>
> If I'd a cow that gave such milk
> I'd dress her in the finest silk.
>
> I'd milk her forty times a day
> And feed her on the finest hay.
>
> If whiskey were a river and I were a duck
> I'd swim to the bottom and never come up.
>
> Oh whiskey drove my mother mad,
> Whiskey killed my poor old dad.

Sometimes I heard sea songs at concerts or parties and they had been tidied up and made more sense than Daddy's versions. This one, however, had me puzzled in any version, but it was fast and tuneful and I liked it:

> In Amsterdam there lived a maid,
> Mark well what I do say,
> And she was mistress of her trade,
> And she was mistress of her trade.
>
> I'll go no more a-roving with you, fair maid,
> A-roving, a-roving, since roving's been my *ru-i-in*,
> I'll go no more a-roving with you, fair maid.

Sad, isn't it? I wonder if *she* ever knew why? Which reminds me of another fragment:

I'll go to sea no more,
I'll go to sea no more.
Oh, I'll marry a wife and have all night in
And I'll go to sea no more.

And then there was the end of the voyage:

I thought I heard the old man say
"Leave her, Johnny, leave her.
Tomorrow you will get your pay
And it's time for us to leave her."

. . . The gear is bad and the mate's gone mad,
And it's time for us to leave her.

Besides all the real chanteys there was a wealth of short songs and verses, cries and sayings from an infinite number of sources. Again I don't always know spelling or names, for an aural memory, as much as sixty-five years old, is what I have to go on. One song which (I think) was a later one had a cockney accent and an irregular rhythm:

My old man's a s'ilor on a carley float
Wiv 'is gorblimey collar and 'is gorblimey coat.
Ties 'is bleedin' muffler round 'is bleedin' froat——Oh,
My old man's a s'iler on a carley float.

Another scrap, this one certainly from World War I, was:

And teach us how to foil the Hun
With paravane and six-inch gun.

A longer song that Daddy sang remained with me in part:

Up then spake our little cabin boy

And a gallant lad was he.
"I've a father and mother in far Bristol town
And tonight they'll be weeping for me, for me,
    for me,
And tonight they'll be weeping for me."

For the raging seas did roar and the stormy winds
    did blow
And we jolly sailormen were setting up aloft
And the landlubbers lying down below, below, below,
And the landlubbers lying down below.

Also concerned in this tragic story were a number of
grown-ups, but their fate failed to move us like that of the
little cabin boy and his parents.

Another cabin boy whose sad tale wrung our hearts was
the one who sailed on the *Golden Vanity*. One of our little
maids asked Mother for the words to this for she wanted
to sing it at a wedding. *We* thought it much too sad. It
went this way:

There was a gallant ship sailed on the Lowland Sea
And the name of the ship was the Golden Vanitee,
And they feared she would be sunk by the Turkish
    enemy
That sailed upon the Lowland, Lowland,
That sailed upon the Lowland Sea.

Then the Captain had a bright idea; he would send his little
cabin boy to bore a hole in the enemy ship and sink her.
He promised:

"Oh I will give you silver and I will give you gold
And I will give my daughter your bride for to be."

So the little cabin boy swam to the enemy ship and bored the hole but when he came back exhausted they refused to pull him aboard, so he:

> . . .drifted with the tide
> And perished in the Lowland, Lowland,
> And perished in the Lowland Sea.

Another little cabin boy I knew of was the one in Captain Marryat's *Mr. Midshipman Easy* (I think) to whom his commanding officer said, "Oh, I see — the fool of the family sent to sea." And he replied, "Oh, no, sir, no, sir, things have changed, sir, since *your* day."

And:

> Captain to cabin boy: "How's the barometer?"
> Cabin boy: "Rising, sir, steadily rising."
> Captain: "And my brandy?"
> Cabin boy: "Falling, sir, steadily falling."

Another constant theme was that of food, for young sailors were often hungry, like those on the Yankee ship that came down East River who dined on "water soup but slightly thinner." Daddy had two recipes for soup which I pass on:

> Soupe de Bouillon: 4 quarts of water and One On-i-on.

> Pea Soup: If you want the soup thick, leave the pea in.
> If you want the soup thin, leave the pea out.

Mother, who hated the sea, had her own thoughts about soup:

Soup, soup, beautiful soup,
Staff of my life it is soup.
If the cheese is past eating
Just coat it with Keating
And shove it all into the soup.

And there was:

Salt beef, salt beef is our relief,
Salt beef and biscuit bread-O,

and:

Sailormen what sail the seas
And keep the laws, and live on yellow peas.

Like many sailors, my father was a reader and also like
most he read his favourites over and over again. Rudyard
Kipling was his idol and we children knew Kipling from
our earliest days. I got *The Second Jungle Book* in 1915
when I was seven and not before I knew the *Just So Stories*
and the first *Jungle Book* off by heart. Our childhood
favourite with a sea theme was "The White Seal's Lullaby":

Oh hush thee my baby, the night is behind us
And dark are the waters that sparkled so green.
The moon o'er the combers looks downward to find us
At rest in the hollows that rustle between.
Where billow meets billow there soft be thy pillow.
Ah weary wee flipperling, curl at thine ease.
No storm shall wake thee nor shark overtake thee,
Asleep in the arms of the slow swelling seas.

(My brother and I both sing this to the tune of "The Day
Thou Gavest, Lord, Is Ended" but neither of us remembers
where we heard this tune to it.)

Another we liked was:

> When the cabin portholes are dark and green
> Because of the seas outside,
> And the ship goes wop with a wiggle between
> And the steward falls into the soup tureen
> And the trunks begin to slide,
> When Nursey lies on the floor in a heap
> And Mummy tells you to let her sleep,
> And you aren't waked or washed or dressed,
> Why then you may know if you haven't guessed
> That you're fifty north and forty west.

We also knew and enjoyed the adult Kipling songs of the sea: ones like "The Liner She's a Lady" or "Loud Sang the Souls of the Jolly Jolly Mariners," or "McAndrew's Hymn" with its "Mr. McAndrew, don't you think steam spoils romance at sea?" or Daddy's motto, which applies even more to our plastic age than it did to his: "Wangartie at the worst and damn all patent fuel."

My father went to sea under sail, travelling in sailing ships up the Miramichi, out to Australia, and around the Horn ("Around Cape Horn and home again, that is the sailor's way.") By the time he got married on a June morning in 1906 he was sailing in steamers of the Ulster Steamship Company, the Head Line. The Head Line ships were called for the headlands of the Irish coast: the Rathlin Head, the Bengore Head, the Fanad Head, the Ramore Head, the Ballgally Head, etc. They had on their funnels the Red Hand of Ulster with its three drops of blood, and a considerable body of local song and story had grown up about them.

A short ferry ride from Larne lay Islandmagee where the men farmed their land and went to sea when the crops were in. Here are some Head Line verses (not complete)

sung to the tune of "It's Five Miles from Bangor to Donaghadee":

> There's a spot in the North that's not far from
>   Belfast
> Where the farmers in summer serve under the mast.
> It's a fine place for making kopecks you can see,
> And the name of that spot it is Islandmagee.
>
> Now aboard the Black Head there's a rum second mate,
> He hasn't a hair on the top of his pate.
> By the size of his feet you can quite plainly see
> That he is a hoocher from Islandmagee.

The next two lines I have forgotten, but this is a tall story
and it ends like this:

> They sailed up the Baltic but the Cape was too wee
> To carry the hoocher from Islandmagee.

Another typical verse of this series is:

> On the hand on the funnel was three drops of blood
> And there up beside it the second mate stood.
> He chipped off one block, "for 'tis sartin," says he
> "We only use two down in Islandmagee."

The sea still laps the Ulster coast but the sailing ships
are gone. The Head Line is all gone too, and on a spring
morning twenty years ago my father flew his Blue Peter
and proceeded to sea. Now I know why the song "Tom's
Gone to Hilo" is so sad, but no one can say that he left
without a trace.

11. The World Around Us

To a Belfast child, Cecil Frances Alexander's familiar hymn, "All Things Bright and Beautiful," seemed to have been written especially for her. This was Nature as we knew it: the heather-covered hills, the small creatures, the skies, the clouds, the sunsets. We looked at the world around and marvelled and sang:

> "The purple-headed mountain,
> The river running by,
> The sunset and the morning
> That lightens up the sky."

The ring of hills was all around us: Cave Hill, Squire's Hill, Divis, Knocklade, and Black Mountain. We watched the crimson rim of the sun sinking behind them, the storm clouds gathering over them, the sun shining out after rain, and the sparkle of rainbows behind them.

Weather was a matter of vital importance to us: a picnic could be ruined by rain, a summer holiday spoiled by icy winds and cold water. We watched the weather and Daddy taught us:

> Dirty days hath September,
> April, June, and November.

All the rest have thirty-one
Without a bloomin' blink of sun.
If any of them had two and thirty
They'd be just as wet and twice as dirty.

He had seen other climes and places, so we were not really surprised at his estimate of summer's prospects:

In the good old summertime,
In the good old summertime,
Strolling round the Opera House
Up to your knees in slime.

We tried chanting:

Rain, rain, go away,
Come again another day,
Little children want to play.
Rain, rain, go away.

Or, more familiar to us:

Rain, rain, go to Spain,
Never show your face again.

We predicted:

Red sky at night, sailor's delight.
Red sky at morning, sailor's warning.
(We didn't know anything about shepherds.)

We told sad tales of uncooperative weather:

Dr. Foster went to Gloucester
In a shower of rain.

He stepped in a puddle right up to his middle
And never went there again.

Or:

Once when little Isabella
Ventured with a big umbrella
Out upon a windy day
She was nearly blown away.

Or:

The wind blew the hairs of my head, Mother,
Two at a time.

It didn't always rain: just enough to keep the grass tender and green, and make the flowers bloom in spring and the little streams run over the pebbles. One of the streams which I never saw was celebrated in a song:

I remember my young days for younger I've been.
I remember my young days by the Muttonburn stream.
It's not marked on a map, it's nowhere to be seen,
A wee river in Ulster, the Muttonburn stream.

Sure the ducks they swim in it, the white and the green,
They muddy the water but they make theirselves clean,
And the ladies from Kerry the finest e'er seen
Come to dunk off their clothes in the Muttonburn
    stream.

Sure 'twill cure all diseases though chronic they've
    been
Just to bathe in the waters of the Muttonburn stream.
Tra la la la la la la, tra la la la la leam,
A wee river in Ulster, the Muttonburn stream.

(The ladies didn't come all the way from Kerry as I supposed, but from Carry: Carrickfergus.)

On clear nights we watched the moon racing by. I loved her then; I love her still. Once, I remember, another little girl and I raced her across the park, and although she barely seemed to move, we couldn't outrun her.

> Lady Moon, Lady Moon, where are you roving?
>   Over the sea.
> Lady Moon, Lady Moon, who are you loving?
>   All that love me.

And:

> O Lady Moon, your horns point to the East.
>   Shine, be increased.
> O Lady Moon, your horns point to the West.
>   Wane, be at rest.

I loved Robert Louis Stevenson's:

> All in a summer afternoon
> I saw a little baby moon,
> And oh I loved its silver shine,
> It was a little friend of mine.

And we learned a little song at school:

> Lady Moon, Lady Moon,
> Sailing up so high,
> Drop down to Baby
> From out yonder sky.
> Babykin, Babykin,
> Far down below,

I hear you calling,
I hear you calling,
I hear you ca-all-ing
But I cannot go.

The Man in the Moon was a cheerful character although I never *saw* him the way I did the Lady. She was a Gibson Girl, with hair like the ladies of my day, and I found her picture in a little book called *Stars Shown to Children*. The man, however, was fun:

The man in the moon came tumbling down
And asked the way to Norwich.
They told him south and he burnt his mouth
With eating cold pease porridge.

There was also a song about an old woman, but not *in* the moon:

There was an old woman went up in a blanket
Ninety times as high as the moon.
"Old woman, old woman, old woman," quoth I,
"Where are you going up so high?"
"To sweep the cobwebs out of the sky."
"May I come with you?" "Yes, bye and bye."

On clear nights we saw stars above us, and Daddy taught us a few of the constellations and the order of the planets around the sun. We chanted: "Men very easily make jugs serve useful needs" — Mercury, Venus, Earth, Mars, Jupiter, Saturn, Uranus, Neptune (no Pluto in *my* day). We also liked:

Twinkle, twinkle, little star,
How I wonder what you are,

Up above the world so high
Like a diamond in the sky.

When the blazing sun is gone,
When he nothing shines upon,
Then you show your little light,
Twinkle, twinkle through the night.

Canadian children wish on the first star of evening. I
don't remember that, but we wished on the new moon
seen over our left shoulders.

One feature of sky and weather that fascinated us was
the rainbow. We had heard that there was a pot of gold at
its foot, but the chances of finding that were too remote
for us to consider. We knew and liked Wordsworth's poem:

My heart leaps up when I behold
A rainbow in the sky.
So was it when my life began,
So is it now I am a man,
So be it when I shall grow old,
Or let me die.
The child is father to the man
And I could wish my days to be
Bound each to each in natural piety.

We found this beautiful but very puzzling. How can the
child be father of the man? Mammy, consulted on the
matter, said it was the same idea as "As the twig is bent so
is the tree inclined." "Oh," we responded, "is it?"

The rainbow, too, had pleasant associations with Noah's
Ark and God's covenant with man. We liked to sing:

The animals came in one by one,

> One more river to cross.
> Said Mrs. Noah, "They'll never be done,"
> One more river to cross.
>
> One more river, and that's the river of Jordan,
> One more river, and that's the river to cross.
>
> The animals came in two by two,
> One more river to cross,
> The elephant and the kangaroo,
> One more river to cross. . . .

The beauty of this song was that the words, except for the chorus, were always different and we could take any liberties we liked with it.

The animals in the Ark and out of it we knew in many nursery rhymes and verses. Noah's Ark had exotic ones, as strange as we pleased, but most of our songs were about familiar friends: the dog, the cat, the horse, the goat, the donkey, birds, and insects and worms.

> Sweet sings the donkey
> As he goes to grass.
> If you don't sing sweetly
> You will be the ass.

(This, for some unaccountable reason, was sung to the loser at "Old Maid.")

> If I had a donkey that wouldn't go
> Do you think I'd wallop him? Oh, no, no.
> I'd tie a juicy carrot right under his nose
> And following it the donkey goes.

141

Horses

If wishes were horses, beggars would ride.

My horse is called Shank's Mare.

> I had a little pony,
> His name was Dapple Grey.
> I lent him to a lady
> To ride a mile away.
> She whipped him and she lashed him,
> She rode him through the mire.
> I wouldn't lend my pony now
> For any lady's hire.
> I wouldn't lend my pony now
> For any lady's hire.

Mammy learnt this when she was a little girl, and both she and Uncle Toe read and recited to us long passages from *John Gilpin*. Uncle Jim, on a Saturday night when he was dummy at a bridge game, would read or sing to us:

> A farmer went trotting upon his grey mare,
>   Bumpety, bumpety, bump!
> With his daughter behind him so rosy and fair,
>   Lumpety, lumpety, lump!
>
> A raven cried "Croak!" and they all tumbled down. . .
> The mare lost her shoe and the farmer his crown. . .
>
> The mischievous raven flew laughing away. . .
> And vowed he would serve them the same
>   the next day. . .

Mother had a very sad song which was confused in my mind with *Black Beauty*:

My clothing it was once of the linsey woolsey wear,
My body it was brushed and they tended me with care,
But now I'm growing old, my beauty doth decay,
My master frowns upon me. Today I heard him say,
"Poor old horse, you must die."

A happier one was:

As I was going by Banbury Cross
I saw a fair lady upon a white horse,
With rings on her fingers and bells on her toes
She shall have music wherever she goes.

Of course, the most romantic was Young Lochinvar who
stole a bride and flung her across his horse and carried her
off. This brought to mind little Lorna Doone, flung across
the big black horse, with her jewelled necklace gleaming,
while John Ridd watched from his hiding place; or Kipling's
"Smuggler's Song":

If you chance to wake at midnight and hear a
     horse's feet,
Don't go drawing back the blind or looking in
     the street.
Them that asks no questions isn't told no lie.
Watch the wall, my darling, while the gentlemen go by.

And we knew:

It's not the 'oppin' over 'edges that 'urts the
     'orses 'oofs.
It's the 'ammer, 'ammer, 'ammer on the 'ard 'igh road
From 'Amstead 'eath to 'Ighgate.

Cats

Some people like cats and others can't stand them, but both groups sing or tell stories about them. Mother sang this sad song, although why we felt such sadness we didn't know; something about the repeated "long time ago," I think.

> Once there was a little kitty
> White, white as snow.
> In the barn she used to frolic,
> Long time ago.

Did Rudyard Kipling start the belief that it was manly to like dogs and hate cats? Certainly this one, from *Just So Stories*, is an anti-cat verse:

> Pussy can sit by the fire and sing,
> Pussy can climb a tree,
> Or play with a silly old cork and string
> To amuse herself, not me.
> But I like Binky, my dog, because
> *He* knows how to behave.
> Binky's the same as the First Friend was
> And I am the man in the cave.

Of course, *everybody* knew:

> I love little pussy, her coat is so warm,
> And if I don't tease her she'll do me no harm,
> So I won't pull her tail or drive her away,
> But Pussy and I very gently will play.

Dogs

Dogs were brave, good, faithful, and altogether worthy characters. We had stories about the St. Bernard who saved mountaineers lost in the snow, and Gelert, the faithful dog put to death by his master and all for a mistake. At school we learned about Poor Dog Tray:

> On the banks of the Shannon when Shelagh was nigh
> No blithe Irish lad was as happy as I.
> No harp like mine could so cheerfully play,
> And wherever I went went my poor dog Tray.

I liked animal songs but they nearly all had an underlying note of sadness. It seemed that animals were born to suffer and die, except, of course, the noisy, nonsensical kind in Daddy's song:

> Where *does* the Rhinoceros
> Get his R-H-I-N-O?
> Why *does* the Hippopotamus
> Not lay an egg like the ostrich does?
> And why *does* the little Ellypant
> Wear one tail behind and another one in front?

Birds

And then there were the birds — particularly robins:

> Robin, robin redbreast,
> O robin dear,
> And robin singing sweetly
> In the falling of the year.

And (*very*) pathetic:

> The north wind doth blow
> And we shall have snow
> And what will the robin do then,
>   Poor thing?
>
> He'll hide in the barn
> And keep himself warm
> And put his head under his wing,
>   Poor thing.

Then there was Uncle Charlie's contribution:

> "Caw caw caw," says the old black crow,
> "Haw hee haw," sings the donkey down below.
> "Chirp chirp chirp," goes the sparrow on the wall
> But divil the note has Hooligan's canary got at all.

Flora

We had flora too, as well as fauna:

> Daffydowndilly
> Has come up to town
> In a yellow petticoat
> And a green gown,

and:

> Ring ting, I wish I were a primrose,
> A bright yellow primrose growing in the spring,
> The stooping bough above me,
> The wandering bee to love me,

The fern and moss to creep across,
And the elm tree for king.

We knew Wordsworth's "Daffodils" and Herrick's "Daffodils" and we learned "My Love's an Arbutus by the Borders of Lene," and we knew (somehow) that Lene was Killarney where Mammy and Daddy went on their honeymoon.

Flowers, like animals, had short lives and sad ones, and unlike dogs were not always what they seemed. Take, for instance, the nettle:

If you gently touch the nettle
It will sting you for your pains.
Grasp it like a man of mettle
And it soft as silk remains.

And roses: everybody knows there's no rose without a thorn except "The Lass of Richmond Hill." We kept hearing, too, of J. M. Barrie who said, "God gave us memories that we might have roses in December."

The white hawthorn or may was another favourite flower; until it bloomed we wore long stockings and winter dresses, for the saying was "Ne'er cast a clout till May is out." The month of May also brought little May Queens, dressed in shabby finery and wreaths of spring wildflowers. They went singing up and down the streets trying to collect a penny or two. One I remember, with a dirty face, a wreath of hawthorn, and singing:

"Ladies I have goldensilver
Ladies I have housenland
Ladies I have ships upon the ocean
All I want is a nice young man."

I knew better. What she really wanted was a penny.

Before we went to school on St. Patrick's Day, Mammy always pinned our little bunches of shamrock on us. This signified that we were Irish and remembered St. Patrick who used the shamrock to teach that God is One in Three. We knew many songs about the shamrock, notably "The Dear Little Shamrock." There was also one of *Moore's Melodies*:

> O the shamrock, the green immortal shamrock,
> Chosen leaf of bard and chief,
> Old Erin's native shamrock.

And then there was:

> Come back to Erin, mavourneen, mavourneen,
> Come back, aroon, to the land of your birth.
> Come with the shamrock and springtime, mavourneen,
> And it's Killarney will ring with our mirth.

We were later to meet this as a song sung to passengers leaving Ireland on shipboard.

One day as I went into a Toronto school, all grown up and far from Ireland, I heard a song that took me back nearly a lifetime. The kindergarten children were singing the song I sang in kindergarten:

> "Come, little leaves," said the wind one day,
> "Come to the meadows with me and play.
> Put on your dresses of red and gold
> For summer is gone and the days grow cold."

Nowadays, the same moon shines on the other side of the world and there's the same lady in it with her Gibson Girl hairdo. Orion still flourishes his club, as he did when my father first showed him to us from a field in Hughenden

Avenue. Spring brings the same rains and birds and flowers. It's just as Wordsworth said:

> So was it when my life began,
> So is it now I am a man,
> So be it when I shall grow old,
>   Or let me die.

Cave Hill, Belfast

*The Belfast docks, with Harland and Wolff's
shipbuilding yards in the background*

12. I'll Sing You a Song but It's All Tommyrot

In my childhood no one discussed such matters as Race, Religion, Sex, and Death with us. Instead, they sang to us constantly; and from the songs we felt we understood what they thought on a great variety of subjects.

My first real experience of learning from a song was poignant and sad. One sunny spring day, Uncle Toe, who was then still a fairly young man, was singing "The Ash Grove." Suddenly I had a picture of old age, of living in the world with all my friends gone, of the loneliness of the old. I ran into the house to hide my tears but, to this day, when I hear these words, my heart bleeds for Uncle Toe, old and bereft:

> My laughter is over, my step loses lightness,
> Old countryside measures steal soft on my ear.
> I only remember the past and its brightness,
> The dear ones I mourn for again gather here.
> From out of the shadows their loving looks greet me
> And wistfully searching the leafy green dome
> I find other faces fond bending to greet me —
> The Ash Grove, the Ash Grove, alone is my home.

The same theme was found in two of *Moore's Melodies* which Mother sang:

Oft in the stilly night
E'er slumber's chains have bound me,
Fond memory brings the light
Of other days around me,

and another one, which I didn't understand but felt, about
a boat that danced on the waves at morning; in the evening
the barque was still there but the waters had gone. It ended
with a desire to be young again:

Give me back, give me back the wild freshness
of morning,
Her clouds and her tears are worth evening's best
light.

We were *not* a musical family, but all sorts of ideas were
embodied in verse and set to a tune that belonged or was
lifted from elsewhere. Events of our day were discussed in
a light-hearted way. Whenever my little brother was faced
with evidence of a disaster like a fire or a collision, he
would shake his head sadly and murmur, "It must be the
suffragettes." And we were familiar with Mendelssohn's
"Spring Song," but only as a vehicle for expressing feelings
about these worthy pioneers:

Put me upon an island where the girls are few,
Put me among the fiercest lions i. .i. .in the Zoo. .oo,
Put me upon a desert and I will not fret,
But for any sake don't put me near a Suffr*a*gette!

"The Soldiers' Chorus" from *Faust* was rendered by Mother
with words like:

Glory and love to the men of old.
Their sons may copy their virtues bold,

Courage at heart and a sword at hand,
Ready to fight and die for Fatherland.

This was pre-war, I suppose, but George Iliff rendered it
thus:

Ham bones and a bully big lump of fat —
My gosh, boys, what do you think of that?

(Even then the idea of fat was disgusting to me, so I forgot
this one.)

On the subject of Music, Daddy had one that expressed
his feelings:

Some talk of Handel and Mozart,
Beethoven too had a very fine art,
But you no can learn their tunes by heart
Like the pibroch played by his nainsel.

For it's hoot and he'll blaw and he'll toot and
he'll stare
With his kilt and his plaid and his twa legs bare
And the ladies smile as they declare,
"He's a fine braw lad, his nainsel."

The organ too may be very good
If it's played to a sanctimonious crowd   *(crood)*
But ye no can say it's half sae good
As a pibroch played by his nainsel.

For it's hoot he'll blaw and he'll toot and he'll stare
With his kilt and his plaid and his twa legs bare
And the ladies smile as they declare,
"He's a fine braw lad, his nainsel."

Mother found some music more than she could bear:

Jane, Jane, your singing's productive of pain,
It jars like the brake of a train,
It rattles like hailstones and rain.
Your vocal vagaries have killed the canaries,
Oh, Jane, Jane, Jane!

Though we were not a musical family, there was a musical accompaniment to everything we did, and the gramophone needed constant winding and changing. Everybody sang: the delivery boys on their bicycles, the little maid polishing the knives or setting the fires, Daddy, Mammy, uncles, and aunts. Where the songs came from I do not know. We had some music books: my grandmother's psalter, with its tunes on top divided from the words, so that you could listen to the announcement and turn: "Psalm Twenty-three, the tune is French." There was also a book, souvenir of a concert, called *The History of the Jubilee Singers with their Songs*, and a small book of Stephen Foster. At school we used *The National Song Book*, with its songs from England, Ireland, Scotland, and Wales, and a collection of *Cries of London*, rounds, and nursery songs. There may have been a few more but these are all I remember, and anything else was transmitted orally.

Every year in the Christmas holidays we were taken to the Pantomime by Uncle Toe. This was his Christmas present to his sisters and brothers and their families. We went in our best new Christmas frocks and sat in the Dress Circle where even the youngest could see, and we oohed and aahed at the First Act Curtain and the unbelievable Grand Finale. To Mother's distress, we also picked up a number of songs, jokes, and banter:

1st Clown   I saw a girl come down a hill.
2nd Clown   Riding on a bicycle.

1st Clown	She fell off at the bottom, you see.
2nd Clown	Yesterday I kissed your wife.
1st Clown	That's *terrible*!
2nd Clown	No, it isn't. She asked me to.
1st Clown	I don't mean that. I mean it doesn't rhyme. Make it rhyme, try again. . . . She fell off at the bottom, you see.
2nd Clown	And I saw the lady's ling-er-*ee*.

Loud laughter from the Dress Circle but Mother was indignant. One pantomime song that she suppressed was "Sergeant Michael Cassidy," but I can only remember a line or so:

> Assidy, assidy, Sergeant Michael Cassidy,
> He's the boy, a wonderful sagacity,
> Sergeant Michael Cassidy.

One that we found very funny (but not because we understood it) was called "The Gypsy Warned Me." We thought Mother had a most unreasonable dislike of it:

> The Gypsy warned me, the Gypsy warned me.
> "Oh," she said to me, "my child,
> He's a bad lad, a very bad lad,"
> But I only blushed and smiled.
> He took me to the country once,
> It really was sublime.
> A dragonfly flew down my neck,
> And what a pantomime!
> For he tried to find out where the flies go
> In the wintertime,
> 'Cos I didn't take the Gypsy's warning.

Mother would have nothing to do with this song, but she

did answer the riddle for us: "Where do flies go in the wintertime?" — "To the glass factory to be made into bluebottles." *And* she taught us another pantomime song:

> Where do flies go in the wintertime?
> Do they go to Gay Paree?
> When they've finished buzzing round our beef and ham,
> When they've finished jazzing on our raspberry jam,
> Do they clear like swallows every year
> To a distant foreign clime?
> Tell me, tell me, where do flies go
> *In* the winter*time*?

The sentimental songs of the pantomime left us cold. We adored the Principal Boy, who was really a girl dressed in blue satin; and the Principal Girl, dressed in pink. They sang their duet, Centre Front, but the songs themselves were boring to us, although they often brought a great round of applause from the house. We preferred the raucous shrieks of the Widow Twanky, Aladdin's mother, as she went to the Public Baths and came rushing on stage, carrying a dripping sponge and demanding: "Who's been boiling cabbages in my bath?" She was, of course, played by a man, and she sang songs like "The Gypsy Warned Me" and others that Mother didn't care for. There were choruses too in the panto with stirring marching tunes like "Tipperary," and "Pack Up Your Troubles." And one song I considered eminently sensible that I think came from pantomime was:

> 'Tis a frantic, most romantic, silly sort of thing
> *That* a royal King, to the man who found the ring
> Should give his daughter, and no matter, be he good
>   or bad,
> Should think that daughter really oughter say that
>   she was glad.

157

Two more disapproved songs which we first learned in pantomime were:

> Things that are naughty are nice to do,
> Nice to do, nice to do,
> Things that are naughty are nice to do
> So let's be nice and naughty.

And:

> The worse you are the more the ladies love you,
> The more they want to hang around.
> Never mind the more precise girls,
> It's the bad lads that get the nice girls.
> Squeeze them all and don't forget to tell them
> All the horrible things you do,
> And just like the ivy that clings to the ruin,
> All the girls will cling to you.

Grown-ups had very strange ideas about what was funny and what was not. For instance, Mother and Aunt Kathleen and Uncle Hubert and even Uncle Toe sang a song we found pitiful, but they said it was nonsense:

> The sun was setting, slowly setting,
> Setting as it never sat before.
> We were feeling tired, very tired,
> So we sat on the baby on the shore.
> > Yes, we sat on the baby on the shore,
> > A thing we had never done before.
> > If you meet the mother tell her gently
> > That we're sitting on her baby on the shore.
>
> The moon was rising, slowly rising,
> Rising as it never rose before.
> We were feeling tired, very tired,

So we left the baby on the shore.
    Yes, we left the baby on the shore,
    A thing we had never done before.
    If you meet the mother tell her gently
    That we left the baby on the shore.

Equally bewildering was the apparently funny fate of Clementine: why our heartless uncles laughed at this we couldn't imagine:

    Ruby lips above the water
    Blowing bubbles large and fine,

or:

    How I missed her, how I missed her,
    How I missed my Clementine,
    Till I kissed her little sister
    And forgot my Clementine.

Also hilarious to the adult but tragic to us was:

    "Oh stay," the maiden said, "and rest"
        Upidee, upidah,
    "Thy weary head upon this breast."
        Upidee, idah.
    A tear stood in his bright blue eye
    But still he answered with a sigh,
        Upidee, idee, idee,
        Upidee, upidah,
        Upidee, upidee, idee,
        Upidee, idah.

Then there was the one that astonished the ladies at school when I sang it to them. Miss Hanna had told us that the next day we would learn "The Village Blacksmith" and

I said cheerfully, "Oh, I know that, my daddy taught me":

> Under the spreading chestnut tree
> The village smithy stands, and he
> Is strong as glue and he owes not a sou.
> Week in, week out, he toils as a rule
> And children coming home from school
> Play larks with the sparks and make rude remarks.

> He goes to church on Sunday
> The choir to admire.
> He loves to hear his daughter sing.
> Toiling, rejoicing, sorrowing,
> He goes to repose,
> And that's the village blacksmith.

Mother sang a number of really sad songs, but not to the uncles who would, no doubt, have laughed at these too. Many of them were about love and death, but my memory of them all is fragmentary, probably because they were not understood. Terrible, but obscure, was "The Four Marys":

> Last night there were four Marys
> And tonight there'll be but three —
> There was Mary Beaton, and Mary Seaton,
> And Mary Carmichael and me,

and:

> They'll tie a napkin round my head
> And they'll no let me see to dee.

And then there was a self-abasing one which went:

> I was not half worthy *of* you,

Not half worthy, my Douglas, of you,
But I'll be so tender, so loving, Douglas,
Douglas, tender and true.

And a really sentimental one:

Fair as a lily, joyous and free,
Light of our prairie home was she.
Everyone who knew her felt the gentle power
Of Rosalie the prairie flower.

Or one, of which only a line or two remains, suggesting
always to me a wet, grey, wintry street at evening and a
tired shawly lady singing:

There are many sad and lonely
In this pleasant world of ours,
Calling ever through the twilight,
"Won't you buy my pretty flowers?"

She also sang the sad tale of "The Babes in the Wood":

Oh say, don't you know how a long time ago
Two poor little children whose names I don't know
Were stolen away on a fine summer's day
And left in the woods, so I've heard people say.
    Poor babes in the wood,
    Poor babes in the wood,
    Oh, don't you remember
    The babes in the wood?

But all Mother's songs were not sad. She also taught us a
Bible song with a surprise ending:

There were three Jews called Patriarchs,
There were three Jews called Patriarchs,

Patri-atri archs, archs, archs,
Patri-atri archs.
There were three Jews called Patriarchs.

The first one's name was Ab-ra-ham. . .
The second one's name was Is-a-ac. . .
The third one's name was Ja-a-cob. . .
These Jews went to Jerusalem. . .
I don't care if they went to Jericho. . .

And she enlivened the classics of our day with irreverent verse:

Poor old Robinson Crusoe,
Poor old Robinson Crusoe.
They made him a coat of an old nanny goat,
I wonder how they could do so,

and:

I've discovered a glorious wrinkle,
Never wake up for twenty years.
Glorious glorious Rip Van Winkle
Never woke up for twenty years.

At family gatherings there was always singing. Uncle Jim won at whist, they say, because of his irritating habit of singing unfinished snatches of songs like "Danube . . . so blue . . . so blue . . . so . . . blue. . . . Come on, Jamesiebald, play one and look at the rest"; or "Sing ho, sing hey, for a merry merry merry maid!" Uncle Doddy, another of Mother's brothers, whose name was John or Johnny, had one "turn" for these occasions. He sang "The West's Awake" with real gusto, becoming quite purple in the face on nothing but strong tea:

"But oh, let man learn liber*tee*
From crashing wave and swelling sea,"

and finished with "We'll watch till death for Erin's sake."
For some reason, this performance both alarmed and fas-
cinated me. I preferred my gentler uncles, Uncle Toe or
Uncle Jay, who sang:

Let Erin remember the days of old
E'er her faithless sons betrayed her,
When Malachi wore the collar of gold,
Which he won from her proud invader.
When her kings with standards of green unfurled
Led the Red Branch knights into danger,
E'er the brightest gem of the Western World
Was set in the crown of a stranger.

Another of their favourites was "The Bard of Armagh" to
a tune also used for "The Streets of Laredo":

Oh list to the tale of a poor Irish harper
And scorn not the notes from his poor withered hand.
Time was when his fingers they might have moved
    sharper
To raise up the praise of his dear native land. . .

And when Sergeant Death in his bright arms shall
    fold me
Lull me to sleep with sweet "Erin Go Bragh,"
By the side of sweet Kathleen my young wife
    they'll lay me
And forget Phelim Brady, the Bard of Armagh.

Like children today, we also learned songs by having our
older friends and cousins pick out the tunes "by ear" on

the piano (this was even before the days of the ukulele). In this way we met most of Stephen Foster's best-known songs, and a number of hymns. These were not the kind we learned in Sunday School (which were, for the most part, the metrical versions of the Psalms and a few paraphrases). These casual hymns picked out by older children were of a kind that might be called semi-sacred. For instance, I thought

> "And He walks with me and He talks with me
> And He tells me I am his own"

was the same kind of song as "Roaming in the Gloaming."

To this group also belonged "Shall We Gather at the River?" and "In the Sweet Bye and Bye we shall meet on that bew-ti-ful shore." Mother also sang this in French but I can remember only "Dans les cieux, dans les cieux."

Then there was a "semi-sacred" song called, I think, "Jerusalem," to which our irreverent uncles taught us a different set of words:

> I wore my Pappy's pants
> To the Easter Monday Ball.
> They were too long
> So I rolled them up,
> And I heard the people call:
> He's a-losin' 'em! He's a-losin' 'em!
> He's a-losin' his Pappy's pants!
> He's a-losin' 'em! He's a-losin' 'em!
> He's a-losin' his Pappy's pants.

All around us, especially from 1914 on, there was a great variety of "popular" songs mostly of the "jingo" kind:

> We've got a navy, the British navy,

To keep our foes at bay.
Our old song "Britannia rules the waves"
We still may sing today.
We've got a navy, a fighting navy,
And our neighbours know it too,
And it keeps them in their place
When they know they've got to face
Those lively little lads in navy blue,

and:

We're soldiers of the Queen, m'lads,
Who've been, m'lads, and seen, m'lads,
In the fight for England's glory, lads,
When we've got to show them what we mean,
And when we say we've always won
And when they ask us how it's done
We proudly point to every one
Of England's Soldiers of the Queen.

To these Daddy added Kipling's "Fuzzy Wuzzy" and "The Absent-Minded Beggar," and school singing class added "The British Grenadiers," the national songs of Our Brave Allies, and "The Bay of Biscay."

Besides the annual Christmas pantomime, we were occasionally taken to plays, anything that was considered suitable for children. We saw "Uncle Tom's Cabin" with little Eva joining the Heavenly Choir suspended from a perfectly visible wire; and "Peter Pan," which I liked, but not as well as the book. Its only song that I can remember was:

Yoho, yoho, the frisky plank —
You walks along it so,
Till it goes down and you goes down
Too tooralooralo.

In summertime there were Pierrots on the sands with the same kind of songs as the Pantomime but none of the glamour. There was once a Punch and Judy show but my strongest memory of it is not wanting to give up my penny to a stranger passing a hat around.

Then there was "La Poupée"! I don't know how old I was, but young enough to believe the whole romantic story. This was my first taste of a kind of entertainment which, years later, Gilbert and Sullivan and the Ballet Russe were to supply. It was the story of a young monk who was heir to a rich inheritance if he was married by his twenty-first birthday. A doll-maker was commissioned to make a life-sized doll which walked and talked, and the young man would marry that and secure his inheritance for the sake of the poverty-stricken order to which he belonged. Unfortunately, the doll-maker was not ready in time and the monk, all unknowing, was married to the doll-maker's real, live daughter. This was, to me, a totally satisfying plot, and I remember yet the song of the abbot, a very sympathetic "uncle-like" character:

> A jovial monk am I,
> Contented with my lot.
> The world without my gates I flout
> Nor care for it one jot.
> Shall I make life dull and dreary
> Because a sombre garb I wear,
> Or have a heart that's light and cheery
> And can afford to laugh at care?
> > A contented mind is a blessing kind
> > And a merry heart is a purse well-lined,
> > So what care I, let the world go by,
> > It's better far to laugh than cry.   *(Repeat)*

> And still I can admire
> Although a monk am I

The witty jest, the song that's best
Or laughter ringing high,
And for all life's young beginners
This would the right prescription be:
Be neither saints nor downright sinners
But make the best of life like me.
    Chorus (*but I think it's a little bit different*)

I was interested in this, and Mother taught me another
about a friar which I thought was about my dear friend
and hero, Friar Tuck:

I am a friar of orders grey
And down the valley I take my way.
I pull not blackberry, haw, nor hip,
Good store of venison fills my scrip,
My long bead-roll I merrily chant,
Wherever I go no money I want,
Wherever I go no money I want,
And why I'm so plump the reason I'll tell,
Who leads a good life is sure to live well.

    What baron or squire or knight of the shire
    Lives half so well as a holy friar,
    Lives half so well, lives half so well,
    Lives half so well as a holy friar,
    As a ho-o-o-o-oly, ho-o-o-oly, ho-o-o-o-oly friar,
    Lives half so well as a holy friar?

And after supper of Heaven I dream
But that is fat pullets and clotted cream.
My self-denial I mortify
With a dainty bit of warden pie.
I'm clothed in sackcloth for my sin,
With old sack wine I'm lined within,
With old sack wine I'm lined within,

The chirping cup is my matin song
And the vesper bell is my whole ding dong.
   Chorus

(I always thought warden pie was game pie but in a Shakespeare class many years later I found it was pears.)

Uncle John Porter in Dublin introduced us to "The Vicar of Bray" but I was much older before the meanings of his efforts to obtain preferment were clear to me. We much preferred that genial soul, Father O'Flynn:

> Of priests we can offer a charming variety
> Far renowned for larnin' and piety.
> Still, I'd advance you without impropriety
> Father O'Flynn as the flower of them all.
> Here's a health to you, Father O'Flynn,
> Slainthe and slainthe and slainthe again,
> Powerfulest preacher and tenderest teacher
> And kindliest creature in all Donegal.
>
> You can talk of your Provost and fellows of Trinity
> Famous forever at Greek and Latinity,
> Faix and the Divil and all the Divinity,
> Father O'Flynn would make hares of them all.
> Come, I'll venture to give you my word
> Never the likes of his logic was heard —
> Down from mythology into theology,
> Prompt at conchology if he'd the call.
>
> Och, Father O'Flynn, you've a wonderful way
>   with you,
> All the old sinners are dying to pray with you,
> All the young childer are wild for to play with you,
> You've such a way with you, Father avick.
> Still, for all you're so gentle a soul,

Yet you've your flock in the grandest control,
Checking the crazy ones, coaxing on aisy ones,
Lifting the lazy ones on with a stick.

And though quite avoiding all foolish frivolity,
Still at all seasons of innocent jollity
Where was the playboy could claim an equality
At comicality, Father, with you.
Once the Bishop looked grave at your jest
Till this remark sent him off with the rest,
"Is it leave gaiety all to the laity?
Cannot the clergy be Irishmen too?"

In spite of the Pantomime, the Pierrots, the Hippodrome,
and the street, it was from our parents that we got most of
our songs. Daddy had, quite literally, a song for everything,
and Mother wasn't far behind. As we polished our shoes or
oiled the cricket bat, he would burst out with:

"All along of dirtiness, all along of mess,
All along of doing things rather more or less,
All along of abby-nay, kul and hazar-ho,
Mind you keep your rifle and yourself just so."

In a quiet moment for a bit of entertainment, we might
get any of a couple of dozen verses of that old song with
its chorus of "How would you, how would you like to be
me?"

I'll sing you a song but it's all tommyrot —
Perhaps you'll remember that I'm off my dot,
But I often have heard people say with a smirk
To be dotty is better than going to work.
   Chorus: Toorooloo, toorolee,
            How would you, how would you like
            to be me?

The other day I called on Miss Brown.
She was taking a bath and she couldn't come down.
I said, "Slip on something, come down just a tick."
She slipped on the soap and came down like a brick.
  Chorus

At dinner one day I said, "Waiter, please,
Would you kindly oblige by removing this cheese?"
"It's good cheese," he replied. "Very likely," I said,
"It may be all right but it's eating my bread."

The sound of wind roaring around the house might bring:

Loud roared the dreadful thunder,
The rain a deluge showered,
The masts were rent asunder
By Lightning's vivid powers.
The night was dull and dark,
Our poor devoted bark,
There she lay all that day
In the Bay of Biscay-O.

Or a cry from the music halls which I'm sure I have incorrectly but I probably heard it wrongly too:

Oh the thunder and the lightning and the hail
    and the snow
And the rain and the wind and the baby falling
    down the stairs.

Rude and whining children were reproved from Kipling:

When you climb out of bed with a frowsly head
And a snarly yarly voice,
When you shiver and scowl and you grunt
    and you growl

At your bath and your books and your toys,
There should be a corner for me-ee-e
And I know there is one for you
When you get the hump,
Camelious hump,
The hump that is black and blue.

Cries of "Not fair" or mild mutiny met with:

If you stop to think what your wages will be
Or how they will clothe you and feed you,
Willy, my son, don't go on the sea
For the sea will never need you.

Mother's face, as she cleared up after a cigar-smoking
party, brought:

Maggie my wife at fifty,
Grey and dour and old,
With never another Maggie
To be purchased for love or gold
. . . . *(forgotten lines)*
For a woman's only a woman
But a good cigar is a smoke.

(Be it said in this connection that my father believed in
each cleaning up his own mess and young guests who left
cigarette butts in the bottom of a coffee cup were severely
reprimanded.)

And this was chanted at my Auntie Dot who came from
Crossmaglen:

In Carrickmacross and Crossmaglen
There are more rogues than honest men.

One great cry of exultation picked up from South American religious processions (but totally misunderstood) was: "O Gloriosa O Stabat Mater!" (This, to me, is still the ultimate in fervent delight.)

And then, of course, there was the song that summed up the way of the world:

> When you smoke a bad cigar there's nothing to do
>   but cough,
> When you're trying to ride your bike there's nowhere
>   to fall but off.
> There's no use trying to make a hen lay anything else
>   but eggs,
> And when you get your stockings on there's nothing
>   inside but legs.
>
> > Nothing! Nothing! Nothing, alas, alack!
> > It makes me wild when I go out: there's nowhere
> >   to go but back.
>
> What's the use of your optics when there's nothing
>   to see but sights?
> When it's getting dark there's nothing to light
>   but lights.
> Something always troubles me, I've always wondered
>   why
> When you get to the end of your life there's nothing
>   to do but die.
>
> > Nothing! Nothing! Nothing, I wonder why
> > When you get to the end of your life there's
> >   nothing to do but die.

A muddy road brought forth the following solemn chant:

We've now arrived, thanks be to God,
Through pathways dark and muddy,
A certain sign that making roads
Is not this people's study,
And though I'm not with scripture crammed,
I'm sure the Good Book says
That hapless sinners will be damned
Unless they mend their ways.

And there were two maxims that ruled our lives:

The Church and State may gang tae Hell
And I'll gang to my dearie O,

and:

It's a poor heart that never rejoices.

And one song, which my father never taught me but I
learned from Mother and *Pilgrim's Progress*, was descrip-
tive of my father:

Hobgoblin nor foul fiend
Shall daunt his spirit,

nor, I think, mine, for my childhood was full of song, not
musical, but stirring, irreverent, and to the point.

13. Where the Alleyman Won't Catch Me

Like Katherine Tynan:

> I was born under a kind star
> In a green world withouten any war,

and the first six years of my life were spent with war as a concept that involved only "The Grand Old Duke of York," "Are You Ready for a Fight for We Are Roman Soldiers," and the great rush of sparks up the chimney as we sat by the fire after tea and Mother read us stories. "Oh, Mammy, look!" we would cry. "Soldiers in the fire."

The concept of patriotism was equally vague. I knew I was Irish for I had learned to sing:

> Oh, my father and mother are Irish
> And I am Irish too.
> I bought a wee fiddle for ninepence
> And it was Irish too,
> And I'm up in the morning early
> Before the break of day,
> And on my wee brown fiddle
> Many's the tune I play,   *(mostly pronounced chune)*

and I realized that my lines had fallen unto me in pleasant
places, like the boy who was born in Ballyjamesduff:

> My mother has told me that when I was born,
> The day that I first saw the light
> I looked down the street on that very first morn
> And gave a loud crow of delight.
> Now most other babies born into this world,
> They whimper, they cry, or they squall,
> But I knew I was born in Ballyjamesduff
> And I lay there and smiled at them all.

As our St. Patrick's Day shamrock was pinned on us, we
sang:

> The *dear* little shamrock,
> The *sweet* little shamrock,
> The dear-little-sweet-little shamrock
> Of *Ireland*.

We had a little maid called Katy who came from Newry.
She was young, rosy-cheeked, bright, and quick. She took
us for a walk in the afternoons and I remember meeting
other children in the park, with their uniformed Nanny.
She said something to Katy, who replied with a toss of her
head and a loving hand on our shoulders, "Irish — and
proud of it too!" I wasn't quite sure what this meant, but
if Katy thought it was a good thing it surely was. There
was another song about being Irish, full of spelling, that
went like this:

> H, A, double R, I, GAN spells Harrigan!
> Proud of the Irish blood that's in me,
> Divil the wan can say a word agin me.
> H, A, double R, I, GAN, you see

> If you want to know the man who can lend
> > a bob or spend a bob,
> It's Harrigan! That's me!

One Christmas I was given a book called *Pixie O'Shaughnessy*, which was about a little Irish girl. Its author was a Mrs. George de Horne Vaizey, a peculiar name, you must admit, but she seemed to think being Irish was peculiar. I couldn't understand it. We had a friend called Dorothy, a pleasant, rather shy little girl, but we were very sorry for her because her mother wore pointed-toed shoes and talked Englishy.

At school I learned:

> Little Indian, Sioux, or Crow,
> Little frosty Eskimo,
> Little Turk or Japanee,
> Don't you wish that you were me?

This seemed a very sensible poem, but years later when Daddy taught us another rather like it, I understood:

> Father and Mother and me,
> Sister and Auntie say,
> People who do like us are We,
> Everyone else is They,
> And They live over the sea
> But We live over the way,
> Yet isn't it shocking that They look at Us
> As a simply disgusting They.

Even in being Irish there were qualifications. We came from the North and, as everyone knows, the North is best. Bagpipes, heard on the street and in the hills, proclaimed one favourite theme:

Cock a doodle, cock a doodle,
I'm the cock of the north.
Cock a doodle, cock a doodle,
I'm the cock of the north.

Later we were to learn the sort of "Patriotic" verse or
song that stresses the superiority of one's own kind. Two
that I remember are:

Kitchener from Kerry, all Irish through and through,
An Irishman was Wellington who won at Waterloo.
Never let yourself forget that you are Irish too,

and:

Pat he may be foolish and very often wrong.
Pat has got a temper but it don't last long.
Pat is fond of jollity and everybody knows
That you'll seldom find a coward where the
    shamrock grows.

And Uncle Charlie assured us:

"You may talk about your King's Guards, Scots
    Greys an' a',
You may talk about your kilties and the gallant
    Forty-Twa,
Or of any other regiment that bears the King's
    command,
But the South Down Militia is the Terror of the Land."

But once in a while there was a trace of doubt:

Bad luck to this marching,
Pipeclayin' and starchin',

How nate one must be to be kilt by the French!
Och I like "Garryowen"
When I hear it at home
But it ain't half so sweet when you're going to be kilt.

At school, with its Quaker background, this sort of patriotism was unknown, although our attention was drawn to our countrymen as "local" authors and heroes. When I was about seven, the whole school read "The Deserted Village," and we found the place of the village on the map. As St. Patrick's Day drew near we noted Slemish where St. Patrick was a herdboy, and once or twice the whole school went to Downpatrick and saw places hallowed by Ireland's patron saint. My memories of the expedition are very faint and have more to do with ginger ale — and the price of it — than with history.

William Allingham was another "local" as we learned "Up the Airy Mountain," which made a great impression upon my childhood. I saw the mountain, of course, as Cave Hill. The verse I liked best was about the stolen child:

They stole little Bridget
For seven years long;
When she came back
Her friends were all gone.
They took her lightly back
Between the night and morrow,
They thought that she was fast asleep
But she was dead with sorrow.
They have kept her ever since
Deep within the lake
On a bed of flag leaves
Watching till she wake.

This was my first realization that beauty and sadness

often belong together. Soon afterwards we learned W. B. Yeats' "The Stolen Child":

> Away with us he's going,
> The solemn-eyed.
> He'll hear no more the lowing
> Of calves on the warm hillside,
> Or the kettle on the hob
> Sing peace into his breast
> Or see the brown mice bob
> Round and round the oatmeal chest,
> For he comes, the human child,
> To the woods and waters wild
> With a fairy, hand in hand,
> For the world's more full of weeping
> Than he can understand.

Many years later, in my teens, I came upon Charlotte Mew, and W. B. Yeats' "Land of Heart's Desire," and also books of Irish fairy tales. They gave me a strong sense of *déjà vu* and a nostalgia for the small schoolroom where I first encountered this wild magic.

I'm glad I was born as long ago as I was, "in a green land withouten any war." Before World War I broke out in 1914, I had time to grow into the secure ways of peace. My mind may tell me otherwise, but deep inside me the basic convictions still hold strong: that Right can never be overthrown by Might, that Truth will prevail, and that God still sits up there keeping an eye on His creation.

In spite of all that, World War I came, and nothing was ever quite the same again. Fear invaded our peaceful hills and the concept of Death was not to be avoided. Even little children were killed in France and Belgium, and in England a Zeppelin bombed children on a bright afternoon as they walked to Sunday School. The ranks of uncles became depleted as they went off to war. Uniforms were everywhere in the streets (Uncle Charlie had *spurs*), and ladies appeared with little boxes of bright flags on pins.

"What are they, Mammy?"

"It's a Flag Day, dear."

"Well, can I buy some for my model ship I'm making?"

"You can buy *one*."

"How much does it cost?"

"Whatever you have. Tuppence would do."

"Well I have a whole sixpence. Can I have a Union Jack and a French one and a brave little Belgium?"

"No, dear, only *one*."

"Why?"

"You're not *buying* the flags, you're *giving* the money to send comforts to the troops."

Then we saw a picture of "Charlie Chaplin in the Trenches" and we learned about the need for "comforts." We cried because of Uncle Harry, who, like Charlie, might have an itchy back and cold feet and be sitting in a pool of water. We bounced our balls to:

Oh, the moon shines bright on Charlie Chaplin,
His boots are cracking for want of blacking,
And his little baggy trousers they need mending
Before we send him to the Dardanelles.

The arch-enemy was The Kaiser. He wore a helmet with plumes and it was he, personally, who sent out the U-boats and the Zeppelins. Once I saw his shadow on my bedroom wall and I nearly screamed the house down. (I have never found out what made it.) I changed my teddy's name from William Henry (after Uncle Harry) to something more respectable, and steadfastly refused to divulge to my

friends what the W in Uncle Harry's name stood for. And
we sang:

> "Kaiser Bill
> Went up the hill"

(but I can't remember what happened to him), and:

> "Little Tirpitz has lost his ships
> And doesn't know where to find them.
> They're bottled up safe in the Kiel canal
> With a British fleet behind them.

And later:

> "How they giggled, how they laughed,
> How the sailors of the Grant Fleet chaffed
> When they heard their Admiral declare
> 'You can land your bally German fleet right there.' "

(I still don't know what this means.)

All this bravado was fine, but what about Uncle Harry?
At home he had always been cold; he used his cup of tea
to warm his cold hands, and now he was in the trenches
like Charlie Chaplin, being bitten by rats and something
called "cooties," and hungry and wet. We sent him "comforts": chocolates and cigarettes and Keating's powder and
little disposable undershirts made of cheesecloth which
Mother made in large quantities on the machine. But what
if he were killed? We knew a terrible song:

> I want to go home
> Where the Alleyman won't catch me. *(i.e., Allemand)*

181

I'll cry, "I don't want to die."
I want to go home.
Far over the sea
Where the Alleyman won't catch me.

And to the tune of "What a Friend We Have in Jesus," we sang:

"When this ruddy war is over
Oh how happy I will be!
When I get my civvy clothes on,
No more soldiering for me."

Then there was:

Oh, it's a lovely war!
What do we want with eggs and ham
When we've got plum and apple jam?
Form fours, right turn,
What do we do with the money we earn?
Oh, it's a lovely war!

And another that went:

If you want the Sergeant-Major
I know where he is, I know where he is,
I know where he is!
Down in the deep dugout
I saw him, I saw him,
Down in the deep dugout I saw him,
Down in the deep dugout.

But the poor private soldier, our Uncle Harry, not young, one of Carson's enlisted men to avoid conscription in Ulster (and all *that* was quite incomprehensible), was:

Hanging on the old barbed wire,
I saw him, I saw him,
Hanging on the old barbed wire, I saw him,
Hanging on the old barbed wire.

And now even little children like Paddy, instead of singing "The Grand Old Duke of York," had a song like this:

"Form fours to the right," said the Sergeant.
"Beer, beer, beer," cried the Privates,
"Merry merry men are we,
For there's none there are that can compare
With the men of the OTC."

But when Uncle Harry came home on leave, he taught us a very comforting and reassuring song:

Old soldiers never die,
They simply fade away.

We weren't quite sure just what happened to old soldiers but as death was all around us now, it was comforting to know that he, at least, was safe from it. Children turned up in school in the mornings with mysterious black bands sewn around their sleeves; blinds were lowered in houses that we passed.
"What does it mean, Mammy?"
"Their brother was killed, dear."
"At the Front?"
"Yes, well, not exactly. He died of wounds."
Then there was a lady in heavy mourning at a holiday place where we went one spring after we had been sick. Her husband was "missing, presumed dead" and no one really explained to us what that meant. Every night before she went to bed she ate something strange called marrow

on toast, and to this day the mere mention of marrow recalls to me this bewildering rite.

One night we were wakened to come downstairs and greet our friends, the younger children of Captain Moore, who had called with the news that their father was found and safe after his ship was torpedoed.

Now, gradually, the war songs stopped being funny. They still urged us to be brave and cheerful, to look for silver linings, whatever those were, but there was a new element in them: anger and hatred. Whether the songs were different or I was older, I am not sure from this distance, but there was less bombast:

> "Where are the boys of the village tonight?
> Where are the lads we knew?
> In Piccadilly or Leicester Square?"
> "Not there, my child, no, not there.
> They have gone for a trip to the continong
> With their rifles and their bayonets bright
> To quell a mad dog's mania, avenge the *Lusitania*,
> That's where they are tonight."

Instead of "Chu Chin Chow," we now marched to "Colonel Bogey," "Tipperary," or "The Old Contemptibles," and advised our friends to:

> "Pack up your troubles in your old kit bag
> And smile, smile, smile!
> While you've a Lucifer to light your fag,
> Smile, boys, that's the style.
> What's the use of worrying?
> It never was worth while,
> So-ooooo — Pack up your troubles in your old kit bag
> And *Smile, Smile, Smile*."

Another less cheerful and more sentimental one was:

> Keep the home fires burning
> While our hearts are yearning;
> Though our lads are far away
> They dream of home.
> There's a silver lining
> Through the dark cloud shining;
> Turn the dark cloud inside out   *(How?)*
> Till the boys come home.

And — not as funny as it seemed at first:

> Good-bye-ee, don't cry-ee,
> There's a silver lining in the sky-ee.
> Bonsoir, Old Thing, cheerio, chin chin,
> Napoo, tiddlyoo, good-bye-ee.

"Blighty" was more cheerful. It suggested a soon-to-come and permanent leave:

> Take me back to dear old Blighty,
> Put me on the train for London town.
> Take me over there, drop me anywhere,
> Liverpool, Leeds, or Birmingham, I don't care.
> I should like to see my best girl —
> Cuddling up agin' me soon she'll be — oh!
> Iddledy, iddledy ighty, carry me back to Blighty,
> Blighty is the place for me.

Then more troubles, long seething, unknown to us children, erupted, and trouble at home became as pressing as trouble at the Front. No one really attempted to explain these things to us. I knew, for instance, that Uncle Harry,

185

who was one of our older uncles, was "at the Front" because of the need for volunteers in Ulster. I knew that not all the children at school wore shamrocks on St. Patrick's Day. I knew Orange Parades but had never really seen a big one, more, I gathered later, because Mother was afraid of crowds and violence than because we were opposed to them.

Mother was certainly opposed to the drums on the hills at night, but it was an unpopular view, for the song said:

> There's times I think the Lord himself
> Must take a skeely down
> To listen to His own wee drums,
> The drums of County Down.

I now know a lot of Orange songs, but I only knew a few scraps when I was a child:

> — O my lily O,
> O my lily O,
> My loyal, loyal
> Orange lily O.

> — On the green grassy slopes of the Boyne
> Where the brave with King Willyum did join
> It's the Blue and the Orange forever
> On the green grassy slopes of the Boyne.

> — *Up* comes a man with a shovel in his hand
> Saying, "Boys, you'll get no faarder.
> King Willyum has a rope
> And he'll hang the Bloody Pope
> E'er ever he'll cross Boyne Water."

Of all that I picked up on the street at this time, one

186

verse remains half forgotten in my mind, and I suppose
the reason I have forgotten is that I didn't understand it
at all:

> Hold the fort for Balfour's coming,
> See he comes and saves.
> Keep the Union Banner flying —
> Britannia rules the waves!

We now had curfew and armoured cars in the streets. If
we left a cricket bat or a scooter outside, we were afraid to
open the garden gate and go and get it. Our big cousins in
Dublin went to "Curfew Parties" where you arrived just
before curfew time and stayed for breakfast.

About this time, too, we became aware of Americans. A
large percentage of our books had always been from the
United States. I read *The Wide, Wide World* and *Queechy*
and *Little Women* and *What Katy Did* and, of course, *Tom
Sawyer*. At school we had a lot of Whittier and the poets
of New England. My mother remembers that when she was
a little girl, one of her uncles complained to her father that
Emerson's *Essays* were "dangerous stuff" to leave for the
young to read. I never thought of the children in these
books as different. They were more like us in their home
life and their thinking than were the schoolgirl heroines of
Angela Brazil or my beloved secret reading, Bessie Bunter.
(If I spent my pocket money on Bessie Bunter, I didn't get
any more.) These Americans or Yankees, as they were
called, arrived as soldiers, and were rich and very boastful
and brought mosquitoes with them, as if our own little
midges weren't bother enough. And we learned rude songs
on the streets, like:

> That's why they're called doughboys;
> It took them so long to rise,

and:

> The Yanks are coming over
> Now it's over over there.

Then there was a more complimentary one, probably American in origin, with our old enemy the Kaiser in it:

> The Russians are rushing the Prussians,
> The Prussians are crushing the Russians,
> Rasputin's disputin' and Italy's hootin',
> The Balkans are balking, Turkey is squawking,
> But God I am thanking the Yanks started yanking
> And yanked Kaiser Bill up a tree.

Long after the war, we continued to sing of the Yanks and their part in it:

> Mademoiselle from Armentières, parlez-voo?
> Mademoiselle from Armentières, parlez-voo?
> We'll soon forget the shots and shells,
> We'll never forget the mademoiselles,
> Inky pinky parlez-voo.
>
> What has become of inky pinky parlez-voo?
> Oh what has become of all the little cooties too?
> Many a cootie has come from France
> In an army shirt or a pair of pants,
> Inky pinky parlez-voo.

And Daddy said:

> Amorous mademoiselle to soldier: "Je t'adore."
> Soldier to Mademoiselle: "Shut it yourself."

The next disaster to strike was The Flu. We heard about it, how everyone was sick and there weren't enough doctors to go around, and people were dying, men, women, and children. Then one Sunday I crouched inside the grate because I was so cold, and my little brother was upstairs in bed very sick with the flu. By evening I was tucked into bed too, and I knew I was really sick because the bedroom fire was lit, a sure sign.

Strangely enough, we had always joined happily in singing that parody of "Good-bye-ee":

"Bonsoir, Old Thing,
Cheerio, chin, chin,
Napoo, take the flu
And die-ee."

But no thought of dying ever entered my head, just chills, misery, beef-tea, and at last a cold November day when I was out again and Billy the Bun came driving down Hughenden Avenue in his cart. My little brother was still very sick in bed so Bill's was a new and welcome face. But he had no time for me that morning. "Go get your mammy, there's a good girl," he said. So I ran and brought her to hear his news. It was good news indeed, for that day was November 11, 1918, and the Armistice had just been signed.

Peace was not at all what we had expected. The soldiers took *ages* to come home, and then we gathered there was no work for them. Some things were better: for instance, at dancing class there was a party and the whole class of well-behaved little girls and boys, in their best clothes and curls, followed a waiter with a tray, just as if he were a Pied Piper, for the tray was filled with little cakes *with icing* . . . something most of us couldn't even remember. Now we could sing:

189

"When the War is over, we shall have some jam,
We shall have some jam, we shall have some jam,
When the War is over, we shall have some jam,
We shall have some Jam!
For You-ou, for Me-ee-ee,
A pot of Tickler's Ja-a-am,
A pot of Tickler's Jam."

Everything was very confusing. For instance, the Germans wanted to come to England. Or did they?

Oh, I am as happy, as happy can be,
There's no one so happy as my Fritz and me,
For when the War's over to Old England we'll run —
Oh, God bless Old England, the Home of the Hun.

And the Americans wanted to stop honest sailormen and the British in general from having a *drink*. The song said:

Mr. Pussyfoot, bow wow,
Mr. Pussyfoot, miaou, miaou.
Fahncy coming from America to try
To make Old England dry.
Mr. Pussyfoot, bow wow.

Then much, much later (grown-ups are *peculiar*) we had something called Peace Day. We gathered firewood and lit bonfires in the streets, but they never seemed as big as we had hoped. There was a Parade that went on and on, and we learned a lot more War Songs, like "There's a Long, Long Trail A-Winding" and "Roses Are Blooming in Picardy" and so on, and more and more war veterans went round and round looking for jobs, some of them far, far away to places like Australia or Manitoba, and there were songs like:

There's a man, man, man in Manitoba
Lonely, so lonely,
There's a man, man, man in Manitoba
And to him you have pledged your word.
There's a man, man, man in Manitoba
Slaving and saving,
Building a nest in the far off West
For his own little English bird,

or:

Arawana on me honour I'll take care of you.
I'll be kind and true. We can bill and coo.
In a wigwam built of shamrock green
We'll make those Redmen smile
When you're Mistress Barney, heap much Carney,
From Killarney's Isle.

The War was over, but childhood was nearly over too, and soon we came to a new land and learned new songs, and even the old songs sung here were just a little bit different. Little by little we became at home in this strange country, and the old one receded and moved farther and farther away. Only now that I am old, older than Mammy and the uncles were then, it all comes back and I am again that little girl who wrote on the pavement:

Alice Kane is my name,
Ireland is my nation,
Belfast is my dwelling place
And school's my occupation.

Notes and References

The following notes comment on the various rhymes, songs, and sayings in each chapter in the order in which they appear. The first part of each item is capitalized to make it easy to locate. References to similar items found in other sources are indicated by the names of the collectors or editors whose books appear in the bibliography. When more than one book by the same author is listed, the author's name alone indicates the first book; other books by that author are indicated by a key word (e.g., Opie, 175 refers to page 175 in The Oxford Dictionary of Nursery Rhymes by Iona and Peter Opie; Opie, Lore, 90 refers to page 90 in The Lore and Language of School-children). Roman numerals refer to volumes, Arabic numerals to pages (e.g. Randolph I, 44 refers to page 44 in Volume I of Vance Randolph's Ozark Folksongs).

If the songs have been recorded by traditional singers, the recordings are listed following the references to printed sources; these are identified by the company name, record number, and location of the song: for example, B8 indicates Side 2, Band 8.

I have not tried for complete documentation of very common items but have cited enough references to indicate their popularity and distribution. I have emphasized book references and cited articles only when book references were missing or scanty, except for Irish items where I have tried to be as complete as possible. Where numerous references have already been compiled in such volumes as Abrahams' Dictionary of Jump-Rope Rhymes, Abrahams' and Rankin's Dictionary of Counting-Out Rhymes, Bronson's The Traditional Tunes of the Child Ballads, Coffin's The Popular Ballad in America, and Laws' American Ballads from British Broadsides, I have not duplicated their listings but have added any additional references I have found.

— Edith Fowke

1. A CHIP OFF THE OLD BLOCK

Most of the "truths" provided by Great-Grandfather and the aunts are familiar sayings recorded in *The Oxford Dictionary of English Proverbs* edited by F. P. Wilson: A SOFT ANSWER, 750; SAVE YOUR BREATH, 418; PRIDE GOETH BEFORE A FALL, 647; TELL THE TRUTH, 807; EARLY TO BED AND EARLY TO RISE, 211. The last is also a nursery rhyme (Opie, 126).

HERE COME I, BEELZEBUB and HERE COME I, LITTLE DEVIL DOUBT turn up in various texts of mummers' plays: for example, in the one from County Antrim in Gailey's *Irish Folk Drama* (43-50), and as separate verses among children (Halliwell, 146; Shaw, 87).

BOYS O BOYS and IF YOU WEREN'T SO BALLYMENA are peculiar to Northern Ireland: the first is reported by Bell (93) and Maggi Peirce knew both of them (41, 29). Ballymena, Ballymoney, Ballycastle and Ballyholme are all towns in Ulster.

ON THE BANKS OF THE STREAM is the first verse of a ballad (usually titled "The Banks of the Clyde" or "The Lad in the Scotch Brigade") which dates from the British war in the Sudan in the 1880s. It was popular in the British army (Winstock, 251), was traditional in Essex (Occomore, 51), and was parodied along the Tyneside (Rutherford, 122).

A BRAVE IRISH SOLDIER turns up in oral tradition in England and Ireland, usually titled "The Banks of the Nile." I have been unable to locate a printed reference.

JACK, JACK, SHOW YOUR LIGHT is a fairly well-known game which the Opies describe (*Games*, 178). They also note A WISE OLD OWL (340), and A TUTOR WHO TOOTED THE FLUTE (*Lore*, 30). Americans also knew the owl (Solomon, 139) and the tutor (Emrich, 199). The tongue twisters are fairly widespread; here are a few sample reports: SISTER SUSIE, Emrich, 199; SHE SELLS SEA SHELLS, Fowke, *Ring*, 62; Turner, 81; THREE GREY GEESE, Baring-Gould, 284; *Handbook*, 682; Tradition TLP 1034-A2; THE LEITH POLICE, Baring-Gould, 284; Opie, *Nursery Rhyme Book*, 157. "Sister Susie Sewing Shirts for Soldiers" by Jack Norworth and "She Sells Seashells on the Seashore" by Wilkie Bard were popular songs early in the century.

IF I WERE A CASSOWARY has turned up in Canada and England (Fowke, 128; Ritchie, 112).

IF I WERE A NIGHT POLICEMAN: An American music-hall singer, R. G. Knowles, wrote a song titled "On the Benches in the Park."

BARBER, BARBER, SHAVE A PIG is a common nursery rhyme (Baring-Gould, 177; Opie, 67), and has been used for counting out (Bolton, 113).

AS IT WAS IN THE BEGINNING is the conclusion of a Kipling poem, "A General Summary" (4).

AH GENTLE DAMES IT GARS ME GREET is a stanza from Robert Burns' "Tam O Shanter."

IT'S AN OLD OLD THING... comes from a Harry Lauder monologue.

2. A MAN, A LADY, AND A BABY

THIS LITTLE PIGGY, which was known as early as 1728, is by far the most popular of the foot and finger plays that parents use with small children (Baring-Gould, 235; Brady, 7; Brown I, 186; Fowke, 100; Fraser, 13; *Handbook*, 681; Northall, 420; Opie, 349; Ritchie, *City*, 7; Sutton-Smith, 183; Withers, 109; etc.).

THIS ONE'S ANDY MARLIN is rare, although a couple of similar rhymes were known in Scotland. One is described as "a rhyme said to a child on the knee, the speaker holding up the legs of the child and using them to represent the persons in this little drama:
    This is John Simson and John Sim.
    He bade him to a feast, and he bade him,
    And they fell out aboot the beef,
    And he owre him and he owre him and he owre him
        and he owre him" (Rymour I, 205).
The other runs:
    This is Willie Walker and that's Tam Sim.
    He ca'd him to a feast and he ca'd him,
    And he stickit him wi' a spit and he stickit him,
    And he owre him and he owre him and he owre him

and he owre him
Till day brak (Macnabb, 3; also Gullen, 8).

THERE WAS A WEE LAMBIE goes to the much-used tune of "Villikens and His Dinah."

WINGY, WANGY resembles the gibberish cited by Bolton (108), and its tune, "Lord, a Little Band and Lowly," is Hymn No. 543 in *The Presbyterian Book of Praise*.

KIND, KIND AND GENTLE IS SHE was composed by T. Richardson. An interesting sidelight: It was sung to Queen Mary by the glass-blowers of Stairport when the King and Queen visited the site of the Cadeby Colliery Mine Disaster in Yorkshire in 1912 (Pope-Hennessy, 685).

TWO LITTLE GIRLS IN BLUE by Charles Graham, published in 1893, has been reported from tradition in the Ozarks (Randolph IV, 338) and was apparently quite popular in Canada as the "Old Favourites" section of the *Family Herald* printed it half a dozen times, the first on 4 September 1926.

LADY, LADY IN THE LAND and similar rhymes about tickling and smiling are widespread (Brown I, 189; Fowke, 102; Fraser, 14; Northall, 307; Opie, 185; etc.).

HEAT THE POKER HOT, HOT, HOT is much rarer, although there are some rather similar Scottish versions. The Rymour Club (I, 124) gives:
> Heat a wummle, heat it well,
> Bore it into Geordie's creel,

while Gregor (150) has several on this pattern:
> Heat a womle, heat a womle,
> Bore a hole, bore, bore, bore,

and Brown (I, 189) gives a North Carolina version that goes:
> Bore a hole, bore a hole,
> Stick a peg, stick a peg.

DIDDLE DIDDLE DUMPLING is a well-known nursery rhyme dating back at least to the eighteenth century (Baring-Gould, 106; Fraser, 7; Opie, 245; Ritchie, 55; etc.). The Opies note that "Diddle diddle diddle Dumpling" was the cry of the hot-dumpling sellers.

THIS IS THE WAY THE BABY RIDES is part of Alice's version of "This Is the Way the Lady Rides" (Opie, 257), which follows the pattern of "Here We Go Round the Mulberry Bush" (Gomme I, 404).

BRIAN O'LINN is a very old and very widespread song that became a nursery rhyme. A "Thom of lyn" was mentioned in the *Complaynt of Scotland* in 1549, and a verse was quoted in a play written about 1560. The hero has many names, Tommy O'Lin or Tam o the Linn, Tom Bolin, and Brian O'Lynn being the most common. It has been suggested that the song was a satire composed by an Englishman to ridicule the Scots (an early form began "Tommy Linn is a Scotchman born"), and later transferred to the Irish. The first verse that Alice gives is the most familiar (although it is usually "his wife's mother") but there are dozens of others. See Baring-Gould, 149; Behan, 12; Belden (who gives additional references), 501; Brown II, 459; Browne, 374; Chambers, 33; Halliwell, 59, 210; Henry, #480; Hoagland, 252; Montgomerie, 111; O'Conor, 64; O Lochlainn, 183; Richards, 61; Walton I, 38; Wehman, 91; Arfolk SB 307-B4; Folk Lyric FL 113-B7; Folktracks FSB 017-A2.

CLAP HANDS! DADDY'S COMING HOME is common in Britain but little known in North America (Brady, 5; Fraser, 13; Gregor, 142; etc.).

DANCE TO YOUR DADDY, a dandling song, is particularly popular in Scotland (Ford, 129; Fraser, 6; Gregor, 150; Halliwell, 81; Montgomerie, 89; Opie, 140; Richards, 52; Columbia ML 204-A2; Tradition TLP 1034-A4).

THERE'S NAE LUCK ABOOT THE HOOSE is a well-known Scottish song sometimes titled "The Sailor's Wife" and usually attributed to Julius Mickle (Graves, 96; Johnson, #44; Stanford, 68).

'TIS A FAMOUS STORY, a Crimean war song, was printed on broadsides in both Ireland and England: "Oh! 'Tis a Famous Story, or Balaclava" by W. S. Fortey of Seven Dials, London, and as "The Charge of the Light Brigade at Balaclava" by Nicholson of Belfast. It has also survived in tradition in both Ireland and England: Sam Henry gives it, saying that he noted the tune "from a man who learnt it from his father, who in his turn learnt it from a Crimean veteran" (#829) and Walter Pardon recorded it on Leader LED 2111.

Roy Palmer reprinted Sam Henry's version (209), and Bill Westaway has recorded a Devon version (Folktracks FSC 60-516-A2).

IT'S A POOR HEART THAT NEVER REJOICES appears in Wilson's *Dictionary of English Proverbs* (638) and Dickens uses it in *Martin Chuzzlewit*.

PLAYING THE GAME IN THE WEST was a popular music-hall song written by Alec Kendall and sung by George Formby, Sr. (MacInnes, 62; Pulling, 35).

JOHNNY GET YOUR GUN is fairly widespread in the British Isles (Brady, 65; Rutherford, 116; Shaw, 48; Folkways 8501-B6).

O PATSY, YOU'RE A VILLAIN is quoted in Molly Hunter's novel, *A Sound of Chariots* (45). The stanza concludes with the lines:
> But when ye're dead upon my soul
> I'll dance upon your grave.

ALL THE GIRLS DECLARE HE'S A GAY OLD STAGER is another music-hall number, "The Galloping Major," written by Fred W. Leigh and George Formby, Sr. and popularized by George Bastow (MacInnes, 80).

MARY HAD A LITTLE LAMB, written in 1830 by Sarah Hale of Boston, is probably the best known of all nursery rhymes (Opie, 299), and it has inspired countless parodies (M. C. Brown, 64, 100; Opie, *Lore*, 90; Peirce, 25; Ritchie, 39; Rutherford, 119; Turner, 96). The pattern of WE'LL SHOVE YOU THROUGH THE WINDOW is common in North American summer camps (Best, 134).

SO MERRY, SO MERRY, SO MERRY ARE WE is the chorus of "The Sailor's Alphabet" (Hugill, 456; Topic 12TS324-B1).

3. OUR DAILY BREAD

PIECE for a children's snack is common throughout the British Isles, but FADGE, BARMBRACK, and CHAMP are typically Irish (*Handbook*, 86-87; McKibbin, 42-43).

MISS FOGARTY'S BEAUTIFUL CAKE (more commonly "Miss Fogarty's Christmas Cake") probably originated in North America. It appeared five times in the "Old Favourites" page of the *Family Herald* where it was attributed to C. Frank Horn (23 April 1913, et al.). It has also been reported from tradition in Pennsylvania, Florida, and Wisconsin (Dean, 43; Morris, 439; Peters, 74). Morris's informant said her father, a sailor, learned it around 1909. Dominic Behan gives a version as "Mrs. Hooligan's Christmas Cake" (57).

MY AUNT JANE is well known in Northern Ireland but not elsewhere (Hammond, 12; O'Hare, 8; Peirce, 46).

THERE WAS AN OLD WOMAN WHO LIVED IN A LAMP is also peculiar to Ireland but less generally known (O'Hare, 15).

THERE WAS AN OLD WOMAN WHO LIVED IN A SINK is more widespread (Baring-Gould, 80; Opie, 430).

WHEN THE QUEEN WANTS A MAN ("Tatties and Herrin'") is Scottish: Buchan and Hall give a traditional version (26), while Ewan MacColl recorded a different form on Prestige INT 13004.

THE POTATOES THEY GROW SMALL (usually "The Praties They Grow Small," sometimes titled "Over There") is known on both sides of the Atlantic. Belden, who gives two Kansas parodies, notes that a sheet-music print of it was issued by Atwill in New York in 1844 with the title of "The Wonderful Song of 'Over There'" (428). In Ireland, where it probably originated during the potato famines of the 1840s, it usually begins "Oh, the praties they are small over here" (Meek, 59; O'Keeffe, 31).

DO YOU WANT A CAR, YOUR HONOUR? ("The Irish Jaunting Car") appears in various Irish songsters (Healy I, 143; Walton II, 35; Wehman, 31); and was apparently popular in Canada as it appeared frequently in the "Old Favourites" (8 June 1927, et al.).

FLOUR OF ENGLAND is a very well-known riddle (Taylor # 1096), appearing in various nursery-rhyme books (Baring-Gould, 273; Opie, 161); and in collections of children's lore (Daiken, 181; Emrich, 26; Fauset, 149).

KING ARTHUR'S PLUM PUDDING and LITTLE JACK HORNER

are familiar nursery rhymes (Opie, 56 and 234). CHRISTMAS IS COMING appears as a nursery rhyme (Baring-Gould, 195) and in many carol collections; Peirce remembers it from her Belfast childhood (42), and Behan from Dublin (Folkways 8501-B2).

AS FOR ME, MY LITTLE BRAIN is from a nineteenth-century American ditty, "Jolly Old St. Nicholas."

SALLY WALKER SELLS FISH is popular in Ireland but little known elsewhere (Brady, 176; O'Hare, 5; Peirce, 29). The only English report I found was from Durham (Rutherford, 117), where Sally suffered a sex change, becoming "Johnny Walker."

IN DUBLIN'S FAIR CITY, known as "Cockles and Mussels," or "Molly Malone," is widely popular (Buck, 167; Hoagland, 256; Walton I, 9); Lady Nairne's CALLER HERRIN' is less frequently heard (Graves, 115; Stanford, 98).

ONE, TWO, THREE, MOTHER CAUGHT A FLEA is often used for counting out and has turned up as a skipping rhyme beginning "O dear me." It is very well known throughout the British Isles but not in America. It seems particularly popular in Ireland (Brady, 59; Daiken, *Out Goes She*, 32; Peirce, 20; Tradition TLP 1034-A5); and quite common in Britain and New Zealand (Douglas, 52; Holbrook, 122; Opie, *Lore*, 19; Rymour I, 20; Shaw, 4, 71; Sutton-Smith, 89, 133).

Brady gives another Irish version of TOSS THE BLANKET (34), and O'Hare has DULSE AND YELLOWMAN under the title of "The Auld Lammas Fair" (13). The latter is part of a longer song written by John McAuley.

NEEVY, NEEVY, NICK NACK is another that is well known in Britain, particularly in Scotland, but not in America. It is very old: the Opies cite a Scottish and north-country reference from 1585 and one in Scott's *St. Ronan's Well* in 1824 (198). It is sometimes used as a game, and occasionally for counting out (Bolton, 115); and a report in the *Miscellanea of the Rymour Club* tells of its use as an arbiter when two boys quarrel (III, 137). See also Ford, 73; Fraser, 29; Gomme I, 410; Gullen, 128; *Handbook*, 676; Montgomerie, 57; Ritchie, *Golden City*, 5; Sutton-Smith, 59.

THE YOUNG SHE LEADS WITH INNOCENCE is from the Scottish paraphrase, "O Happy Is the Man Who Hears," by Michael Bruce (1746-1767); it is Hymn No. 127 in *The Presbyterian Book of Praise*.

OPEN YOUR MOUTH AND SHUT YOUR EYES is a rhyme I remember from my Saskatchewan childhood (Fowke, 124). Brady gives another Irish version (22), and Brown has three from North Carolina (I, 202).

4. WATCH FOR BICYCLES

For various children's insults see Opie, *Lore*, 170-72, and Knapp, 38-75. In Protestant Ulster TORY was a disparaging term, implying Jacobite sentiments. FARDEN, derived from farthing, meant tiny. Brady reports SHAKE HANDS, BROTHER, from Dublin (6). SPECKLED FOUR EYES is fairly widespread: Daiken heard it in Dublin (*Out Goes She*, 37) and the Knapps report it from America (66). GINGER, YOU'RE BALMY is heard in England (Opie, *Lore*, 170; Ritchie, 76).

The pattern of ALICE KANE IS MY NAME is used variously as autograph or flyleaf rhyme, or occasionally for skipping. Probably the most famous form is the one James Joyce (15) incorporated in *Portrait of the Artist as a Young Man*:
> Stephen Dedalus is my name,
> Ireland is my nation,
> Clongowes is my dwelling place,
> And heaven my expectation.

Rutherford (92) gives another Irish version:
> Patrick Murphy is me name,
> Ireland is me nation,
> Dublin is me dwelling place,
> And Home Rule is me expectation.

Chambers (394) and Fraser (134) have it as "Scotland is my nation," Thompson (111) has "England is my nation," and Fraser and Thompson add a rather morbid second verse:
> When I'm dead and in my grave
> And all my bones are rotten
> This little book will remember me

When I am quite forgotten.

Turner (115) gives an Australian variant with a new twist:

Mary Jones is her name,
Single is her station,
Happy be the man
To make the alteration.

The extended ADDRESS does not seem to be reported in collections but its use is widespread. Again Joyce (16) testifies to its popularity in Ireland:

Stephen Dedalus
Class of Elements
Clongowes Wood College
Sallins
County Kildare
Ireland
Europe
The World
The Universe.

FOOLS' NAMES is also familiar, but is rarely reported. It has turned up in Mississippi (M. C. Brown, 82) and Alabama (Solomon, 78).

CRY, BABY, CRY, and COWARDY COWARDY CUSTARD are both common wherever English is spoken (Baring-Gould, 310; Evans, 136; Fowke, 117; Knapp, 61; Lynch, 56; Opie, *Lore*, 188; Sutton-Smith, 132; Turner, 70).

DOES YOUR MAMMY KNOW YOU'RE OUT? is particularly popular in Ireland and northern England but seems little used elsewhere (Brady, 16; Daiken, *Out Goes She*, 37; Peirce, 22; Ritchie, 21; Shaw, 26).

PUT YOUR FINGER IN THE CROW'S NEST is very widely known, in various forms such as foxy's hole, corbies' hole, Tabby's house, and crab's nest (Brown I, 184; Fowke, 103; Gregor, 143; Opie, 175; Peirce, 8; Sutton-Smith, 183; etc.).

ADAM AND EVE AND PINCH ME TIGHT, which is even more widespread, is remarkably consistent wherever it is used, with only a rare exception. Alan Buck (26) remembers a different Irish form:

Pinchme and Punchme went out to swim,
Pinchme was drowned, Who came in?

Alice's Belfast version adds the word "tight" which is unusual: Dorothy Howard also knew it in that form (189). For examples of the usual form, see Baring-Gould, 261; Evans, 140; Fowke, 122; *Handbook*, 678; Lynch, 57; Opie, *Lore*, 59; Turner, 79; Withers, 11; etc.

I WENT INTO THE HOUSE seems to be most familiar among American children (Emrich and Korson, 169; Evans, 14; Newell, 141). Jokes of this type are also international: there are similar Dutch, German, and French versions (Brown I, 172).

OH, WATANNA SIAM: I heard this in Saskatchewan in the 1920s and suspect it is widespread but the only reference found is in Opies' *The Language and Lore of Schoolchildren* (296).

SAMSON'S RIDDLE appears in the 14th chapter of Judges, and SOLOMON CHOOSING THE BABIES is in the 3rd chapter of 1 Kings.

The CATCH AND PUNNING RIDDLES are similar to those the Opies cite in *Lore*, 79-84. The first of the punctuation puzzles, CHARLES THE FIRST, is well known and dates back to 1792 (Baring-Gould, 273; Emrich, 66; Opie, 115; Turner, 79; etc.), but the one about Moses is unusual. BROTHERS AND SISTERS HAVE I NONE is very well known (Baring-Gould, 276; Brown I, 310; Emrich, 57; Fowke, *Ring*, 25; Opie, *Lore*, 367; Turner, 79; etc.).

LONDONDERRY, CORK AND KERRY, a typical catch riddle, is naturally popular in Ireland (Brady, 166; Lynch, 57). ROBIN-A-BOWER is more interesting. It is a true riddle (Taylor #762) found mainly in England where it is known as Arthur O'Bower. The Opies suggest it may refer to King Arthur, and that Bower may be a corruption of the Scottish "bowder," a blast or squall of wind (57). They also note that the earliest record was in a letter from Dorothy Wordsworth in 1804, and that Beatrix Potter quoted it in *Squirrel Nutkin*. A BIG FAT GERMAN resembles the more recent deductive riddle in which a boy and his father are in a car accident, the father is killed, and the boy taken to a hospital where the surgeon exclaims, "I can't operate on him, he's my son."

IT'S A LONG WAY TO BALLYWALTER is a parody of "Tipperary," published by Jack Judge and Harry Williams in 1912. The Opies give a different parody from Scotland (*Lore*, 91).

5. PRO TANTO QUID

Alice's mother's version of WE'RE ALL NODDING has not turned up, but the pattern is widespread. Randolph (IV, 414) gives a Missouri version as a lullaby, and Rich'ardson (60) has a similar one from the Southern Appalachians:

We're all ae noddin'
Nid nid noddin'
An' fallin' off to sleep.

The song "Gudeen to You, Kimmer," which Burns contributed to the *Scots Musical Museum* in 1803 (Johnson, #523), had the chorus:

We're a' noddin, nid nid noddin
And we're a' noddin at our house at hame,

and a notation that it went to the tune of "We're A' Noddin" indicated that the song was already old then. It was known in Canada, for a version appeared several times in "Old Favourites" (31 August 1897, et al.). The pattern suggests that it was the ancestor of the American "Dodger Song" about the characters who were "all dodging, dodging, dodging, all dodging their way through the world" (Botkin, 875).

The verse about A FAIR LITTLE GIRL is "Good Night and Good Morning" by Richard Monckton Milnes, Baron Houghton (1809-1885); it was first published in 1859 and is reprinted in the Opies' *Oxford Book of Children's Verse* (171). It must have been well-established in Irish tradition: Alice's mother learned it in the 1880s and Maggi Peirce remembers it from her childhood some sixty years later (18).

Oliver Goldsmith (1728-1774) was one of the many Irish literary figures whose works were emphasized in Irish schools, and Rudyard Kipling (1865-1936) was very popular in the early years of this century. His verses about schoolmasters, LET US NOW PRAISE FAMOUS MEN, come from "A School Song" which formed the frontispiece to *Stalky and Co.* and was reprinted in his collected verse (556). "Let us all praise famous men and our fathers who begot us" is in the Apocrypha Book of Ecclesiastes.

The rhyme about DR. FOSTER is very widely known in both Britain and America. The Opies (168) note that the earliest version is Francis Douce's counting-out rhyme for which he was "indebted to his pretty little Sister Emily Cory, 1795"; it ends with the lines:

"He had a brave beaver with a fine snout. Stand you there out!"
They also quote an emigrant Irish form from the American *Mother Goose's Quarto* (c. 1825):

John O'Gudgeon was a wild man,
He whipt his children now and then.
When he whipt them he made them dance
Out of Ireland into France.

Halliwell's Scottish version from 1842 features the legendary German magician, Dr. Faustus, making his scholars dance "out of Scotland into France" (41). Later versions give him many pseudonyms: Mr. Foster, Dr. Franklin, Dr. Long, Mr. Dunn, Mr. Smith, Mr. Macpherson, Mr. Drum, Mr. Green, Mr. Low, and Mr. Frog. Abrahams lists versions used for both skipping (38) and counting out (37). Other references include Brady, 98; Brown I, 179; Daiken, *Out Goes She*, 34; Evans, 51; Fowke, 58; Shaw, 11; Sutton-Smith, 55.

FIVE TIMES FIVE came from Alice's father. It is known in the States: Botkin gives it as an Oklahoma version of "Weevily Wheat" in *The American Play-Party Song* (349) and another Oklahoma version in *A Treasury of Western Folklore* (787) which Peggy Seeger recorded on Folkways 2005. However, an earlier form was known in Scotland where it appeared in the *Miscellanea of the Rymour Club* (II, 74).

The Opies note the antiquity of the familiar lament, MULTIPLICATION IS A VEXATION (from a manuscript c. 1570), and give a modern version from Birmingham (*Lore*, 173). It was more familiar in earlier times (Chambers, 393; Halliwell, 167; Northall, 310) than in this century when the emphasis on multiplication tables has declined.

THERE'S NO DEW LEFT ON THE DAISIES AND CLOVER is from Jean Ingelow's poem, "Seven Times One: Exultation," one of her "Songs of Seven" published in *Poems*, 1863.

ONE TWO THREE FOUR FIVE SIX SEVEN, the skipping rhyme that Mammy disliked, is extremely widespread. In New Zealand it also met with disapproval: Sutton-Smith quotes an informant, "I must say that this was rather frowned upon by our Victorian parents as being 'not nice'" (89). In the numerous reports the first two lines are standard but the last two vary greatly. Abrahams cites half a dozen skipping versions (151) and half a hundred counting-out versions (176). The Opies note that it has been current since the

1880s (*Games*, 37). See also Baring-Gould, 249; Brady, 54; M. C. Brown, 34; Fraser, 133; Peirce, 20; Shaw, 73.

BABES CAN COUNT UP BY ALGEBRA: Children's alphabets were very popular at least since the seventeenth century. The Opies give five (47) with many references, and the Baring-Goulds give eight, also with references (242).

The trick riddle about the TWENTY SICK SHEEP turns up in England (Opie, *Lore*, 71); the United States (Brown I, 312); and Canada (Fauset, 164).

AS I WAS GOING TO ST. IVES has been current since 1730 (Opie, 377) and is well known in North America (Brown I, 313; Emrich, 53; Fauset, 152; Knapp, 107; etc.).

THE MAN WHO HAS PLENTY OF GOOD TOBACCO is known on this continent as "The Peanut Song" (Frey, 61).

Walter de la Mare quotes UN, DEUX, TROIS in his anthology, *Come Hither* (684).

ONE, TWO, BUCKLE MY SHOE is the best known of the many counting songs. Abrahams has twenty-two references in *Jump-Rope Rhymes* (149) and nine more in *Counting-Out Rhymes* (174). Bolton gives a version that goes up to "Twenty-nine, thirty, make a kerchy," which he says was used in Massachusetts as early as 1780. The Opies give some early versions (333), and more recent references include Brown I, 169; Emrich, 228; Fraser, 130; *Handbook*, 678; Turner, 52.

ONE TWO THREE FOUR is also widespread: its protagonist is usually Mary but sometimes she becomes Lily, Jennie, Lady, or even "little Freddie." She commonly eats cherries, but occasionally plums or berries, and sometimes the pattern changes to "Two four six eight, Mary at the garden gate." The Opies note a version from about 1815 that added "Nine, ten, eleven, twelve, Peasants oft in ditches delve" (334). It is occasionally used for skipping (Abrahams, 108), but more frequently for counting out: Abrahams and Rankin list thirty-two references (179). See also Brady, 54; Brown I, 165; Fraser, 57; Nicholson, 215; Peirce, 20; Ritchie, 13.

OH, BONEY WAS A WARRIOR is a widely known chantey found in most collections (Hugill, 445).

BONJOUR, MA CHÈRIE comes from a song that was very popular among American as well as British soldiers during World War I; both Dolph (156) and Niles (50) include it, and the latter explains the "Combien, ma chèrie" line: "Voulez-vous couchez avec moi ce soir — oui, combien?"

KILLALOE has been termed "The Great Irish Comic Song." Nicholson of Church Lane, Belfast, printed it on a broadside, but it does not seem to have been picked up in the Irish songsters. John Moulden reports that it was written by Robert Martin of Ross, County Galway, for a Pantomime, "Miss Esmeralda," presented at the London Gaiety Theatre for Christmas, 1887 (Watters and Murtagh, 29, 30, 96). It was apparently popular in Canada, perhaps because we have a Killaloe in northern Ontario: "Old Favourites" printed it seven times, the first on 19 November 1924.

LATIN IS A DEAD LANGUAGE used to be well known before Latin began to disappear as a regular school subject. The Opies cite it (*Lore*, 173), and Turner gives it from Australia (66).

AMO, AMAS apparently springs from a song by John O'Keeffe (1747-1833), an Irish poet and playwright, but it usually turns up in parody forms (Daiken, 86; Shaw, 13).

AFTER VERBS TO REMEMBER: The Opies give the mnemonic for the gender of Latin nouns in *I Saw Esau* (35), and they collected a version of BOYIBUS KISSIBUS dating from about 1910 (letter, 5 February 1981). Chambers has a somewhat similar verse, "Laddibus and lassibus" (157).

NO SURRENDER is an Irish catch phrase dating from the siege of Derry in 1688. Robert Harbison, who calls his book *No Surrender: An Ulster Childhood*, quotes:
> Sir Edward Carson had a cat
> He sat it by the fender,
> And every time it caught a mouse
> It shouted "No Surrender!"   (131)

OH, ROB ROY WAS A TAILOR BOLD: These verses are from a song called "The Irish Schoolmaster" by J. D. Sidey. The Belfast Girl Singers recorded it (Rex 15064), Peirce knew a fragment (24), and a version appeared in "Old Favourites" (28 May 1913).

The Opies give some comments on SCHOOL FOOD and quote a couple of versions of THERE IS A BOARDING SCHOOL (*Lore*, 163 and 88). Peirce learned the song in Ireland (22), Ritchie (42) and Shaw (99) heard it in England, and Randolph (III, 479) in the United States.

6. SALT, MUSTARD, CAYENNE PEPPER

RING-A-RING-A-ROSY is in practically every collection of children's singing games and nursery rhymes over the last century. Despite the legend that it dates back to the Great Plague, the Opies (364) note that "the words have not been found in children's literature before 1881," although Newell (127) cites a possible relative known in Massachusetts about 1790:

Ring a ring a rosie,
A bottle full of posie,
All the girls in our town
Ring for little Josie.

Here is a sampling of the multitudinous references: Baring-Gould, 253; Brady, 12; Brown I, 150; Daiken, 150; Douglas, 59; Fowke, 11; Fraser, 24; *Handbook*, 676; Henry, #48; Gomme I, 108; Northall, 360; Ritchie, *Golden City*, 166.

THE GRAND OLD DUKE OF YORK is almost as popular. The Opies (442) point out that this nineteenth-century slur on Frederick, Duke of York, was a revision of an earlier rhyme about the King of France which dates from the seventeenth century. A Scottish version (Rymour I, 77) celebrates "The Grand Old Duke of New York," and Nicholson (232) suggests another hero:

Napoleon was a general,
He had ten thousand men.

Other references include Baring-Gould, 138; Brown III, 135; Douglas, 36; Fowke, 37; Gomme I, 121; Peirce, 10; Sutton-Smith, 42.

THE CHILD WANTS A NURSE: "The Farmer in the Dell" is another almost universal game. Here is a representative sample: Bolton, 119; Brady, 101; Brown I, 146; Ford, 68; Fowke, 13; Gomme II, 420; Lynch, 52; McMorland, 49; Newell, 129; Folkways 8501-A2.

Unlike the three preceding games which are played throughout the whole English-speaking world, I'M A WEE FILORY MAN is primarily Irish, with some British relatives. Hammond (13) and Peirce (47) give Ulster versions similar to Alice's. In Dublin, Brady (127) has it as "the wee Polony man"; the Baring-Goulds (259) and Opies (*Nursery Rhyme Book*, 132) have it as "Bangalorey Man"; Gomme (I, 129) and Holbrook (117) have "the Gable 'Oary Man"; Gomme also has the "Holy Gabriel," and Hornby (13) has the "Gabel Huntsman." Scottish children sing of the "wee malody man" (*Those Dusty Bluebells*, 30), and it has been suggested that the Gaberlunzie man is another relative.

YOU SHOULD SEE MY COATTAILS FLYING is from "You Should See Me Dance the Polka" sung by George Grossmith, Sr., in 1886. It is quoted in Flora Thompson's *Lark Rise to Candleford* (199).

YIP YIP YIP TOORALIADDY, which went to the tune of "Tread on the Tail of Me Coat," probably dates from the coronation of King Edward VII in 1901.

I WEAR MY PINK PYJAMAS is still current in the United States where it is sung to "The Battle Hymn of the Republic" rather than "The Merry Widow" (Best, 106; Knapp, 174); and it has also turned up in Australia (Lowenstein, 23).

HERE ARE THE ROBBERS COMING THROUGH: This form of the game usually associated with "London Bridge" seems to be most popular in Ireland (Brady, 140; *Handbook*, 675; Lynch, 53; Peirce, 13; Folkways 8501-A2), although it is also known in England (Gomme I, 192; Holbrook, 102), North America (Brown I, 140; Fowke, 31), New Zealand (Sutton-Smith, 33), and the West Indies (Elder, 103).

NUTS IN MAY is thoroughly international as this sampling indicates: Buck, 26; Brown I, 109; Douglas, 51; Fowke, 32; Gomme I, 424; Holbrook, 99; Newell, 89, 236; Nicholson, 340; Randolph III, 373; Sutton-Smith, 36.

PADDY FROM CORK seems to be well known in the British Isles but little known elsewhere (Gomme II, 36; Holbrook, 117; McMorland, 54; Peirce, 11; Shaw, 85). The only North American version I have come across was collected by Leonora M. Pauls from Arthur Rowe of Edmonton in 1981 (personal communication, 25 May, 1981).

WILL YOU GIVE US BREAD AND WINE? This old battle game has long been popular with varying combatants. It began as "The Roman Soldiers," then switched in different localities to tell of the Irish and English, English and French, Yankees and Rebels, or simply "the rovers" and "the gallant soldiers." It is best known in the British Isles but has also turned up in North America (Brady, 112; Brown I, 43; Daiken, 16; Elder, 111; Fowke, 34; Fraser, 95; Gomme II, 343; Gullen, 27; Newell, 248; Nicholson, 119; Columbia SL 206-B1; Folktracks FSC 30-201-A10; Folkways 3565-A4; Tradition TLP 1034-B5).

CAME TO SEE JINNY JO probably originated in Scotland, for "Jo" is the old Scottish name for sweetheart. In England it became Jennie Jones, and other variants include Janet Jo, Georgina, and Jilly Jo. It was very popular in the British Isles: Gomme (I, 260) gives seventeen versions and indicates that she has more, and it has also been fairly widespread in North America. Here is a representative sampling: Brown I, 44 (with additional references); Chambers, 140; Daiken, 136; Ford, 91; Fowke, 32; Fraser, 121; Gullen, 62; *Handbook*, 677; Holbrook, 66; Hornby, 42; Knapp, 148; Newell, 63; Rymour II, 4, 13; Folktracks FSA 60-072-A.

WHAT'S YOUR NAME? This rigmarole seems more common in Britain than in North America. The Opies give a number of versions (*Lore*, 156) and cite a Halliwell "Patchy Dolly" that echoes Alice's mother's version, with a note that Pudding of Thame was the name of the devil in a book of 1603. See also M. C. Brown, 95; Daiken, *Out Goes She*, 10; Fowke, 76; Howard, 231; Shaw, 6; Solomon, 82; Turner, 78.

WE ARE THREE KNIGHTS: Newell points out that early forms of this game were based on the ancient custom of buying a bride and cites similar versions from Germany, France, Italy, and Spain (39). It dates back at least to 1784 when Ritson noted it in *Gammer Gurton's Garland* (15). Old forms usually speak of lords, knights, or brethren; later ones often substitute Jews. It is very well known both in the British Isles and North America (Behan, 89; Chambers,

143; Daiken, 83; Douglas, 37; Evans, 22; Ford, 91; Fowke, 34; Fraser, 113; Ghallchoir, 110; Gomme II, 257; Gullen, 100; *Handbook*, 677; Montgomerie, 72; Rymour I, 76; Shaw, 76; Folktracks FSA 60-072-B; Folkways 8501-A2).

HERE'S AN OLD WOMAN FROM SANDYLAND is extremely common throughout the British Isles but little known in North America. The main variations are in the name: the oldest form seems to have been "Here comes the lady of the land" which later changed to Babyland, Babylon, Barbaryland, or Sandyland. A Scottish version has Sandy's land, an English version, Cumberland, and an Irish version, Sandy Row, after a Belfast street. Gomme suggests the game originated from the practice of hiring servants, with the mother setting forth the qualifications of the children (I, 313). See also Baring-Gould, 256; Brady, 106; Chambers, 136; Daiken, 82; Ford, 91; Fraser, 124; Gullen, 121; *Handbook*, 675; Halliwell, 143; Hornby, 100; Montgomerie, 72; Newell, 56; Rymour II, 3, 72; Thompson, 147; Folktracks 60-072.

KING WILLIAM WAS KING GEORGE'S SON is one of many somewhat similar courtship games. Newell refers to it as a kissing round, although his version does not have the "Kiss and run" tag (73). It is rather strange that this celebration of British royalty should be extremely popular in North America: the Brown collection cites eighteen texts, lists another thirty sent in from North Carolina, and gives references to some thirty others in American sources (Brown I, 113). See also Emrich, 180; Fowke, 24; Gomme I, 302; *Handbook*, 678; Peirce, 12; Randolph III, 344; etc.

NEIGHBOUR, NEIGHBOUR, HOW ART THEE? probably originated with the Quakers in North America: Newell gives a very similar version that circulated in New York and Pennsylvania in the nineteenth century (130). The Opies have a variant in *The Family Book of Nursery Rhymes* (174).

OLD MRS. McQUADE'S DEAD hasn't shown up in the collections checked, but it was obviously played in England around the turn of the century. In Agatha Christie's *Mrs. McGinty's Dead*, Poirot asks Superintendent Spence "How did she die?" and he says:
> Children's game. We used to play it when we were kids. A lot of us in a row. Question and answer all down the line. "Mrs. McGinty's dead." "How did she die?" "Down on one knee just like I." And then the next question, "Mrs. McGinty's dead."

"How did she die?" "Holding her hand out just like I." And there we'd all be, kneeling and our right arms held out stiff. And then you got it. "Mrs. McGinty's dead." "How did she die?" "Like THIS." Smack! The top of the row would roll sideways and down we all went· like a pack of ninepins. . . Takes me back, it does.

Mary Ogilvie describes a similar game, "Queen Anne's Dead," that was played in Scotland in the 1860s: it "consists of children sitting in a row, the first child making the bald statement, 'Queen Anne's dead,' followed by a query from the second child, 'How did she die?' to which the first child replies, 'Shaking one hand, just like I,' and so it continued to the end of the row" (27).

ONE POTATO, TWO POTATOES ranks high in popularity among counting-out rhymes, although it is usually "One potato, two potato, three potato, four" rather than the plural form. Abrahams and Rankin list thirty-five sources (164). See also Brady, 5; M. C. Brown, 12; Holbrook, 123; Lynch, 47; Sutton-Smith, 94; Arts Council LPS 3018-B2.

PIGGY ON THE RAILWAY: The Opies note that this has been current since the beginning of the century, with some versions naming Paddy, Peggy, Polly, Tommy, Sammy, or Teddy. They suggest it stems from an old Scots·ditty, "Pussy at the fireside suppin' up brose" (*Games*, 37). Abrahams lists it in *Counting-Out Rhymes* (189) and *Jump-Rope Rhymes* (159). See also Brady, 11; King, 31; Langstaff, 17; Montgomerie, 115; Turner, 36; Tradition TLP 1034-A4.

NANCY ANN TOOK IT OUT OF THE PAIL: Hugh Shields collected a version of this in South Antrim in 1968 (letter, 25 March 1981) which was also used for playing jacks ("fivestones"):
> Sonsy Ann she won the game,
> She rolled it up in her petticoat tail.
> Good luck, bad luck, in or out,
> If I had a-cheated I would h'a went out.
>   ("Sonsy" meaning fat or contented, or both.)

ONE TWO THREE FOUR FIVE is usually a counting-out rhyme (Abrahams and Rankin, 175), and sometimes used for skipping (Abrahams, 150). See also Baring-Gould, 249; Fraser, 13; Opie, 334; Peirce, 21; Ritchie, *Golden City*, 6.

SALT — MUSTARD — CAYENNE PEPPER is a pattern very wide-spread for skipping, sometimes as "Salt, vinegar, mustard, pepper," "Salt, mustard, ginger, pepper," etc., and often linked with other rhymes such as "Mabel, Mabel set the table," or "Mother sent me to the store" (Abrahams, 175). See also Brady, 78; M. C. Brown, 36; Ritchie, *Golden City*, 137; Turner, 37.

ONE TWO THREE O'LEARY is the Irish form of the rhyme that becomes "alara" or "alora" elsewhere. It is most frequently used for ball-bouncing but sometimes for skipping (Abrahams, 154). A sampling: Daiken, 33; Douglas, 3; Emrich, 138; Fowke, 75; Fraser, 55; Knapp, 6; Peirce, 6; Ritchie, *Golden City*, 80; Folkways 8501-A3.

HOUSE TO LET is widely used for skipping (Abrahams, 66), occasion-ally for counting-out (Abrahams and Rankin, 103), and as a taunt (Northall, 306). See also Fowke, 59; Fraser, 57, 127; Opie, *Lore*, 12; Peirce, 35; *Those Dusty Bluebells*, 28; Turner, 28; Folkways 8501-A3.

TEDDY BEAR, TEDDY BEAR, sometimes with substitutes for Teddy (Ladybird, butterfly, old lady, etc.), is one of the most popular skipping rhymes: Abrahams lists over seventy sources (186). See also Brady, 84; M. C. Brown, 36; Cosbey, 90; Fowke, 49; Peirce 34; Rutherford, 64; Shaw 88; Solomon, 51; Folkways 7029-B11.

GYPSY GYPSY is usually a ball-bouncing rhyme but occasionally used for skipping (Abrahams, 57) and counting out (Abrahams and Rankin, 87). See also Emrich and Korson, 138; Fowke, 74; Ritchie, *Golden City*, 98; Rutherford, 84; Turner, 31; Folkways 7003-A2 (as Indian, Indian).

DIE, DIE, LITTLE DOG, DIE is less common than the previous items and seems to be restricted to the British Isles (Brady, 11; Holbrook, 108).

METHODY BEAT THEM ALL was a cheer used for Belfast's Meth-odist College.

OUR QUEEN WON refers to the May Day celebrations when a Queen was chosen. Maggi Peirce has a similar rhyme from her Ulster childhood (38), and Betty Messenger (196) knew:
    Our Queen won,
    The others had to run.

Hi Ho Hi Ho,
Our Queen won.
For other May Queen rhymes, see Harbison, 35; Opie, *Lore*, 257;
Arts Council LPS 3018-A6.

MY MOTHER TOLD ME is an offshoot of the more widely known
rhyme:
My mother told me
That she would buy me
A rubber dolly....
(See Rutherford, 76, note, and Arts Council LPS 3018-A1.)

AFTER THE BALL is one of the many parodies of Charles K.
Harris's popular song of 1892; for others, see Brady, 176; Opie,
Lore, 91; Ritchie, 121, 132; Rutherford, 105.

ACADEMY BEAT THEM ALL was a cheer for the Belfast Royal
Academy, a co-educational school which Alice attended briefly.

7. COME ALONG TO THE QUEEN'S ARCADE

FOR WHAT WE ARE ABOUT TO EAT: Stan Hugill notes that
"This is a Victorian Navy toast (heard on a Saturday night at sea)
and often referred to by my father, Henry J. Hugill, R.M." (Letter,
9 October 1981.)

CHEER, BOYS, CHEER plays upon the two meanings of "mangle":
a machine for pressing clothes by passing them between two heated
rollers, and a verb meaning to spoil. The rhyme seems to be mainly
Irish: Brady reports it from Dublin (168) and Shaw from Liverpool
(86). It may be an offshoot of a patriotic song, "Cheer, Boys,
Cheer," by C. Mackay and J. H. Russell dating from the Crimean
War (Winstock, 165).

BELFAST, LISBURN ... are the market towns of Antrim listed in
order of size about 1916.

IF I'D AS MUCH MONEY AS I COULD SPEND: The street cry,
"Old Chairs to Mend," appears in various nursery-rhyme books
(Baring-Gould, 98; Halliwell, 86; Opie, 114).

THE SWEETIE SHOP was equally popular among Scottish children as Mrs. Fraser indicates in her chapter on "The Saturday Penny" (159-76).

I'LL SING YOU A GOOD OLD SONG: De la Mare gives this form of "A Fine Old Irish Gentleman" in *Come Hither* (63). It is a slight adaptation of "The Fine Old English Gentleman" that Kidson and Shaw include in *Songs of Britain* (66), noting that it was founded upon an early seventeenth-century song, "The Queen's Old Courtier." It must have been widely known, for Irish songsters have a couple of parodies: "A Good Old Irish Gentleman," and "A Rare Ould Irish Gentleman":

> I'll sing you a dacent song that was made by a Paddy's pate
> Of a rale ould Irish gentleman who had a fine estate,
> Whose mansion it was made of mud, with thatch and all complate
> With a hole through which the top so graceful did retrate.
> Hurrah for the Irish gentleman, the boy of the oulden time
> (Wehman, 69).

There was also an American Mexican War version: "The Fine Old Southern Gentleman" (Dolph, 410).

HARK, HARK, THE DOGS DO BARK is a popular nursery rhyme known as far back as 1784 when it appeared in *Gammer Gurton's Garland* (Ritson, 26). The Opies suggest that it may have been inspired by the wandering beggars of Queen Elizabeth's reign, although tradition holds that it was a Jacobite rhyme ridiculing the Dutchmen who came to the English court in the train of William III in 1688 (152).

COME ALONG TO THE QUEEN'S ARCADE was a local verse adapted from a fairly well-known song, "The Tin Gee-Gee" by Fred Capes (Fraser, 74). It featured the Lowther Arcade in the Strand in London which Pulling notes was "once the Mecca of children taken to buy toys" (141).

TAKE CARE OF THE PENNIES is a familiar proverb (Wilson, 798).

SAVE UP ALL YOUR MONEY is the ending of a song usually called "There Was an Old Soldier" which was popular during the American Civil War (Sandburg, 432) and has survived to the present in Canada and England (Fowke, *Ring*, 91; Shaw, 105).

WHEN THE COAL COMES FROM THE RHONDA is a Welsh parody of "When the Roll Is Called Up Yonder."

THEN SHOUT, BOYS, HURRAY is from a song satirizing the Merchant Shipping Act of 1894 which laid down the rations allowed on shipboard and covered work, fines, and punishments. As one requirement was that sailors must have daily limejuice after a certain number of days at sea, this song was sometimes titled "The Limejuice Ship." (This English method of preventing scurvy among seamen resulted in Americans terming Englishmen "Limeys.") Hugill gives a four-stanza version (58) and Captain H. R. Watson knew it in Australia as "According to the Act" (Wattle Archive Series 2-B9).

LLOYD GEORGE NO DOUBT WHEN HIS LIFE PEGS OUT: This amusing satire circulated among sailors who blamed Lloyd George for the Merchant Shipping Act. Because it set standards for seamen's work, food, etc., those ships which had previously treated their crews more generously cut back the rations to those specified in the Act.

The rhymed parodies of advertisements Alice's mother knew are typical of many such rhymes popular among children (for some American versions, see Knapp, 162-65). FULL MANY A GEM OF PUREST RAZORENE echoes Gray's "Full many a flower is born to blush unseen," and HARK THE HERALD ANGELS SING is widely known (Opie, *Lore*, 89; Turner, 91).

CAN YOU TELL A DONKEY FROM A LEMON? and HOW DO YOU PRONOUNCE CASTORIA? are typical of the catch riddles very popular among children (for other examples, see Opie, *Lore*, 68).

MAMMY, WHY DOES DADDY CALL THAT MAN ONE AND SIX? A bob is English slang for a shilling and a tanner for sixpence: hence Bob Tanner equals one shilling and sixpence — "one and six."

I GAVE McCANN ME CAN is known in Scotland as "The Hole in Me Can" (Buchan, 37). It was particularly popular among Belfast children, for both O'Hare (23) and Peirce (38) remember it.

216

8. I KNOW MY LOVE

APPLE JELLY, JAM TART is typical of the divination rhymes used for skipping all over the English-speaking world. Abrahams lists over sixty similar patterns involving foods in which apples, peaches, strawberry shortcake, ice-cream soda, and black-currant jam seem particularly popular (37). To these may be added two Canadian and two Irish references: Brady, 90; Cosbey, 76; Fowke, 54; Peirce, 34.

OH HAVE YOU BEEN IN LOVE, ME BOYS? Despite Alice's insistence on "murphies," this song's title is "The Garden Where the Praties Grow": it was written by Johnny Patterson (Walton I, 21; Wehman, 25; Intercord Xenophon Int. 181.002-A2).

I KNOW WHERE I'M GOIN' is a very well-known Irish love song which Hughes gives from County Antrim (I, 22). See also Hoagland, 267; O'Keeffe, 85; Peirce, 58; Walton II, 71; Folktracks FSC 45-181-A8.

I'M GOIN' DOWN THE TOWN: Ciaron Carson of the Northern Ireland Arts Council remembers this parody of the above song from his childhood (conversation, 9 March 1981), and the Belfast Girl Singers recorded it as "Darling Jimmy" (Rex 15064). The Irish poet Padric Gregory has published a poem, "Darlin' Jimmy," with the note that it is "based on old folk-song fragments."

I'VE GOT A BONNET TRIMMED WITH BLUE: Hughes reports this from West Kerry as "A Polka Fragment" (IV, 18); McMorland gives a Scottish version (64); and Thompson gives it from England (141).

I KNOW MY LOVE is another popular Irish love song. Hughes, who lists it as "West Irish," notes that in Galway and Clare it was sometimes sung in alternate English and Irish verses (I, 70). See also *Journal of the Irish Folk Song Society*, 1(1904), 52; 2(1905), 24; O'Keeffe, 122; Walton I, 151; Folk Legacy FSE 8-B6.

SHE'S A FINE BIG LUMP OF AN IRISH A-GIR-A-CULTURAL GIRL is widely known as "The Agricultural Irish Girl." O Lochlainn notes that the tune is a hornpipe, "Off to California," and that it was a favourite with all race-goers. He gives a sketch of the lady who used to sing it at the Harcourt Street station on race days and travel on the trains exhorting the passengers, "Don't forget Mary Ann, boys" (*More Irish Street Ballads*, 132). Most versions name the girl Mary Ann Malone rather than the Kitty Sloan of Alice's version (Healy I, 264; Hoagland, 244; O'Keeffe, 98; Walton II, 26; Wehman, 56).

JUMBO SAID TO ALICE is from a music-hall song by Gus Elen and Dan Crawley. The London Zoo sold Jumbo to Barnum's Circus for two thousand pounds in 1882, provoking considerable public protest and inspiring several songs (Pulling, 186).

CHARLIE CHUCK is not very common: Daiken reports it as a skipping song from Dublin (*Out Goes She*, 30), and Withers heard it in the United States (40).

O KATY CONNOR is another music-hall song, by Tom Leamore and Austin Rudd.

JUST JUMP OVER THE GARDEN WALL is from "Over the Garden Wall," by Harry Hunter and G. D. Fox (Browne, 79; Disher, 182). It may have inspired a children's game-song that New Zealand children use for skipping (Sutton-Smith, 106), and Scottish and Irish children for bouncing ball (*Those Dusty Bluebells*, 19; Arts Council LPS 3018-A5).

WILL YOU ACCEPT OF THE KEYS OF MY CHEST? is one form of a widespread answer-back song usually known in Britain as "The Keys of Heaven" or "The Keys of Canterbury," and in America as "Paper of Pins." Some versions end with the girl accepting the keys to the chest and then being repudiated by the suitor; in others, as in Alice's mother's version, she proves true-hearted, with the resulting happy ending. Dean-Smith lists various British forms (82) and Fowke gives a number of other references (*Ring*, #179, 154). See also Tradition TLP 1034-B5.

IMPUDENT BARNEY O'HEA obviously springs from a poem by Samuel Lover (1797-1838), but despite the same title and verse pattern, and some identical lines, Alice's version differs considerably from the original in which the girl finally decides that Barney "has the blarney to make a girl Mistress O'Hea" (Hoagland, 413; O'Conor, 65; Wehman, 71).

DARLING MABEL is a music-hall song by Tom Costello which was popular during the Boer War (Winstock, 246).

HE PROMISED HE'D BUY ME A BASKET OF POSIES is from an old love song usually titled "O Dear, What Can the Matter Be?" or "Johnny's So Long at the Fair." The Opies have traced it back to a manuscript of about 1775 (248). See also Baring-Gould, 118; Brown III, 170; Fowke, *Ring*, 126; etc.

JACK, SELL YOUR FIDDLE appeared in *Gammer Gurton's Garland* in 1784 (Ritson, 24) and was echoed by Burns in his poem about "Rattlin' Roarin' Willie" in 1788 (Johnson, #194). It appears in various nursery-rhyme books (Baring-Gould, 86; Halliwell, 190; Opie, 240); and Hugill quotes a chantey version (361).

ON SATURDAY NIGHT I LOST MY WIFE: Holbrook gives this as "How to Find a Lost Wife" (125); the Opies include it in their *Family Book* (136); and the Rymour Club had a slightly different version (I, 94).

I HEAR SOMEONE WHISTLING is from "The Whistling Thief" by Samuel Lover (Healy I, 267; Henry,#710; O'Conor, 154; Walton II, 28; Wehman, 81; "Old Favourites," 2 December 1913, et al.; Claddagh CC9-B6; Tradition TLP 1004-A10.)

AGAIN AND AGAIN AND AGAIN is one of the best known of the many songs about unholy matrimony, usually with the title "When I Was Single" (Belden, 437; Brown III, 54; Brophy, 66; Fowke, *Ring*, 140; McMorland, 79; Shaw, 106; Folktracks FSC 45-181-A11).

THERE WAS AN OLD FARMER is one of the most popular Child ballads, "The Farmer's Curst Wife" (No. 278). For its numerous versions, see Bronson IV, 180; Coffin, 148 and 275. Some Irish texts: Hayward, *Ulster*, 36; Healy II, 63; and Walton II, 14. For record references, see Fowke, *Traditional Singers*, 213.

AND THEN LOOK OUT FOR SQUALLS is from a music-hall song by Alec Hurley and Daisy Dormer.

DON'T WHISTLE SO LOUD ("Micky O'Dowd") is another music-hall song, by Arthur Lennard.

9. SIMPLE RIGHT AND WRONG

Most of the precepts that guided the Ulster children in the early years of the century were familiar proverbs or lines drawn from hymns in *The Presbyterian Book of Praise*. SPARE THE ROD is universally known (Wilson, 759). THROUGH EACH PERPLEXING PATH OF LIFE is the second paraphrase beginning "O God of Bethel" by Philip Doddridge, Hymn 301. BEHOLD HE THAT KEEPS ISRAEL is a metrical version of the 121st Psalm, "Unto the Hills," also in *The Presbyterian Book of Praise*. FOR WE KNOW THE LORD OF GLORY is from Hymn 543, "Lord, A Little Band and Lowly" which provided the tune for "Wingy, Wangy" in Chapter 2. GOD IS ALWAYS NEAR ME by Philip P. Bliss is Hymn 511.

CLEAN HANDS AND CLEAN FACES is typical of the many moralistic verses intended to cultivate the desired childish manners. The Opies (*Lore*, 47) cite a parallel to TOMORROW WILL BE FRIDAY:
> Friday, pie-day,
> Keep your nose tidy.

BIRDS IN THEIR LITTLE NESTS AGREE by Isaac Watts is one of his *Divine Songs*, No. XVII. WE ARE BUT LITTLE CHILDREN WEAK by Cecil Frances Alexander (1818-1895) is Hymn 527 in *The Presbyterian Book of Praise*. DARE TO BE A DANIEL, by Philip P. Bliss, is Hymn 459; it was popular with both Irish and Scottish children (Fraser, 190; Harbison, 54). WHO IS ON THE LORD'S SIDE? was written by Frances R. Havergal and John Goss, c. 1877. TRUST NO LOVELY FORMS OF PASSION is from a hymn titled "Courage, Brother, Do Not Stumble."

TELL THE TRUTH AND SHAME THE DEVIL is a fairly well-known proverb (Wilson, 807).

SOME SAY THE DIVIL'S DEAD: Chambers gives this as "A Jacobite Rhyme," notes that it went to the tune of "The Birks of Abegeldy," and quotes a paragraph from *Tait's Magazine*: "Sir Walter Scott, when the exciting news burst upon Europe that Bonaparte had miraculously escaped from Elba and was moving on Paris in great force, began a letter to a friend with this snatch of song" (383). See also MacNabb, 4; Montgomerie, 81; Wilson, 181.

MONDAY'S CHILD IS FAIR OF FACE is widely known in slightly varying forms. The Opies cite half a dozen nineteenth-century versions (309). See also Baring-Gould, 218; Brown VI, 24; Emrich and Korson, 98; Fowke, *Ring*, 85; Ritchie, 59; etc.

OH, JENNY BROWN SHE BAKED MY BREAD resembles a stanza in the well-known American song, "Drill, Ye Tarriers, Drill!" which Thomas F. Casey published in 1888.

WAY DOWN YONDER IN YANKETY YANK is an American ditty that Pete Seeger popularized as "May Irwin's Frog Song" (Seeger, 12). A calypso singer, "Blind Blake," recorded his version in the 1950s.

COME TO THAT HAPPY LAND is the original hymn which is better known in its parodied forms: see "There Is a Boarding School" in Chapter 5.

Most of the moral precepts are familiar proverbs listed in Wilson's *Oxford Dictionary of English Proverbs*: SOME THINGS ARE BETTER LEFT UNSAID (cf. 453); A STITCH IN TIME (775); A BAD WORKMAN QUARRELS WITH HIS TOOLS (26); IT'S NOT THE HEN THAT CACKLES (cf. 97); A PLACE FOR EVERYTHING (628); KEEP YOUR EYES AND YOUR EARS OPEN (419).

SOME BOOKS ARE LIES FRAE END TAE END is the first stanza of Burns' poem, "Death and Dr. Hornbook," a satire composed in 1785 about a local schoolteacher who ran a shop where he advertised "Medical advice gratis."

BIBLICAL RIDDLES are now seldom heard but they used to be quite popular. Emrich (76) and the Opies (*Lore*, 85) give samples.

TELL TALE TIT is chanted throughout the whole English-speaking world (Baring-Gould, 36; Brown I, 176; Daiken, *Out Goes She*, 72; Fowke, 116; Lynch, 56; Opie, *Lore*, 189; Peirce, 28; Sutton-Smith, 126; Turner, 77; Folkways 8501-A3; etc.).

Several of the children's precepts are also familiar proverbs that Wilson lists: FINDERS KEEPERS (257); TURNABOUT IS FAIR PLAY (846); FIRST COME, FIRST SERVED (262).

STICK YOUR HEAD IN THE PORRIDGE POT seems to have been peculiar to Northern Ireland: Belfast children were still chanting it some sixty years after Alice heard it (Arts Council LPS 3018-B6).

"I LOVE YOU, MOTHER" is from a poem, "Which Loved Best?" by Joy Allison; it appeared in some early school texts.

"PUDDING AND PIE," SAID JANE appears as "Greedy Jane" in *Another Book of Verse For Children* compiled by E. V. Lucas in 1907; the Opies reprinted it in their *Oxford Book of Children's Verse* (328).

LITTLE POLLY FLINDERS (Opie, 354) and A DILLER, A DOLLAR (Opie, 378) are well-known English nursery rhymes; the latter dates back at least to 1784 when Ritson printed it in *Gammer Gurton's Garland* (23). Ritson also knew "GO TO BED," SAYS SLEEPYHEAD which is still popular on both sides of the Atlantic (Baring-Gould, 82; Brown I, 177; Opie, *Lore*, 390; Peirce, 41; Ritson, 25; Shaw, 124; etc.).

10. THE HAND ON THE FUNNEL

STAR OF PEACE by Jane Cross Simpson (1811-1886) is Hymn No. 494 in *The Presbyterian Book of Praise*.

WHITE WINGS THEY NEVER GROW WEARY is by Banks Winter (Disher, 145).

RISE AND SHINE ON THE BLACK BALL LINE: Stan Hugill discusses the origin of the cry of "Show a leg!" in *Shanties and Sailors' Songs* (18):

> It was the custom of allowing the port wenches aboard that started the well-known turning-out cry of "Show a leg!" The Seamen of those days went barefooted, whereas the women who came aboard sported white cotton stockings. When the bosun's mate made his rounds in the morning to turn the hands to, his cry of "Show a leg!" would produce either a bare calf or a white-stockinged leg — the former having to jump out of their hammocks smartly, the ladies being allowed to lie in.

Most of the chantey fragments turn up in many books so it is probably enough to relate them to Hugill's *Shanties from the Seven Seas*, the single most complete collection. The first lines are followed by Hugill's title and page. OH THE ANCHOR IS WEIGHED, "Rio Grande," 87; IN MOBILE BAY, "Roll the Cotton Down," 152; HEY FOR REUBEN RANZO, "Reuben Ranzo," 240; 'BOUT SHIP'S STATIONS, "Paddy Lay Back," 321; OH TOMMY'S GONE, "Tom's Gone to Hilo," 261; OH WE'LL RANT AND WE'LL ROAR, "Spanish Ladies," 385; A IS THE ANCHOR, "The Sailors' Alphabet," 456; A YANKEE SHIP CAME DOWN EAST RIVER, "Blow, Boys, Blow" in the rather unusual "Harry Tate ship" version, 228; O SALLY BROWN I LOVE YOUR DAUGHTER, "Shenandoah," like Hugill's "Sally Brown" item, 173; OH ONCE I LOVED A YANKEE GIRL, "Haul Away, Joe," 358; WHISKEY IS THE LIFE OF MAN (these stanzas are usually identified with "The Little Brown Jug" and "Rye Whiskey"), "Whiskey Johnny," 274; IN AMSTERDAM THERE LIVED A MAID, "A-Rovin'," 48; I'LL GO TO SEA NO MORE, "Go to Sea No More," 582; I THOUGHT I HEARD THE OLD MAN SAY, "Leave Her, Johnny," 293.

GOD SAVE IRELAND by T. D. Sullivan (1827-1914) is one of many texts set to the tune of George F. Root's American Civil War song, "Tramp, Tramp, Tramp, the Boys Are Marching." The Irish form was written in 1867 to celebrate the Manchester Martyrs (Healy II, 137; Hoagland, 522; Walton I, 107; Wehman, 105). BENEATH THE UNION JACK is a fragment from the "Anti-Fenian Song" composed at the time of the Fenian raids in Canada in 1866 (Fowke and Mills, 104). The same pattern provided a well-known children's rhyme, "Vote, vote, vote for dear old Janie" (see Fowke, 57).

MY OLD MAN'S A S'ILOR is from a music-hall song by George Leyton and Lil Hawthorne.

UP THEN SPAKE OUR LITTLE CABIN BOY comes from "The Mermaid," Child ballad No. 289 (Bronson IV, 370; Coffin, 157, 279); and fragments of it turn up in collections of children's lore (Daiken, 152; Fraser, 106).

THERE WAS A GALLANT SHIP: "The Golden Vanity" is Child No. 286 (Bronson IV, 312; Coffin, 153, 277; for records, see Fowke, *Traditional Singers*, 160).

223

Captain Frederick MARRYATT (1792-1848) wrote a number of popular sea stories including *Mr. Midshipman Easy* (1836).

Compare the PEA SOUP recipe with Maggi Peirce's Belfast saying: "To hell with poverty, put another pea in the soup" (51).

SOUP, SOUP, BEAUTIFUL SOUP is a parody of "Soup" by E. A. Searson, published in 1916 (Gammond, 279).

Alice's father was very fond of Kipling, as his songs indicate. Pages are given for *Rudyard Kipling's Verse*. OH HUSH THEE MY BABY originally appeared in *The Jungle Book* (648); WHEN THE CABIN PORTHOLES ARE DARK AND GREEN is from "How the Whale Got His Throat" in *Just So Stories* (604). THE LINER SHE'S A LADY (158), McANDREW'S HYMN (120), and LOUD SANG THE SOULS OF THE JOLLY JOLLY MARINERS, from "The Last Chanty," (160) were originally published as separate poems. WANGARTIE, mentioned in "McAndrew's Hymn," refers to cheap Australian coal.

Hugill gives AROUND CAPE HORN AND HOME AGAIN as "The Sailor's Way" (387).

THERE'S A SPOT IN THE NORTH is another of the many songs to the ubiquitous tune of "Villikens and His Dinah," best known in Ireland as "Six Miles from Bangor to Donaghadee."

The BLUE PETER mentioned at the end is the navy signal for P, meaning "Proceed to sea."

11. THE WORLD AROUND US

ALL THINGS BRIGHT AND BEAUTIFUL by Cecil Frances Alexander with music by William H. Monk was published in 1848; it is No. 512 in *The Presbyterian Book of Praise*. Recently it has provided the titles for a series of books and television programmes by the Yorkshire veterinarian James Herriot.

DIRTY DAYS HATH SEPTEMBER is a parody of the well-known mnemonic rhyme; the Opies credit a very similar parody to Tom Hood (381).

IN THE GOOD OLD SUMMERTIME parodies the popular minstrel song that Ren Shields and George Evans published in 1902.

RAIN, RAIN, GO AWAY and RAIN, RAIN, GO TO SPAIN are two very old and very well-known rhymes: the Opies cite versions from the seventeenth century (360). A few other sources: Daiken, 175; Fowke, *Ring*, 80; Ritchie, 62; Folkways 3501-A1.

RED SKY AT NIGHT is probably the most common of the weather-forecasting rhymes, often with shepherd in place of sailor (Brown VII, 227; Fowke, *Ring*, 81; Ritchie, 62; Turner, 83; Wilson, 741; etc.).

DR. FOSTER WENT TO GLOUCESTER is widely known today but apparently did not appear in print until 1844. The Opies note that the rhyme of puddle with middle suggests the older form "piddle," and mention a suggestion that it was inspired by Edward I whose horse is said to have been mired in the mud of Gloucester (173). See also Baring-Gould, 88; Bolton, 119; Turner, 89; etc.

ONCE WHEN LITTLE ISABELLA seems to be from a poem, "The Umbrella," by Ann and Jane Taylor.

I REMEMBER MY YOUNG DAYS is a popular Ulster song known as "The Muttonburn Stream" for the river that runs near Carrickfergus (Hayward, 6; Morton 16); in more recent times it has been parodied as "The Moygannon Stream" (O Boyle, 61).

LADY MOON, LADY MOON, WHERE ARE YOU ROVING? is by Richard Monckton Miles, Lord Houghton, and appears in the Opies' *Oxford Book of Children's Verse* (171).

O LADY MOON, YOUR HORNS POINT TO THE EAST is by Christina Rossetti (1830-1890); it appears in De la Mare's *Come Hither* (690) and the Opies' *Book of Children's Verse* (277).

ALL IN A SUMMER AFTERNOON by Robert Louis Stevenson (1850-1894) appeared in *Poems of Many Years* in 1888.

LADY MOON, LADY MOON, SAILING UP SO HIGH was written by Kate Kellogg and appears in Wiggin's *Pinafore Palace* (222).

THE MAN IN THE MOON is a popular nursery rhyme dating from

at least 1784 when it appeared in *Gammer Gurton's Garland* (Ritson, 19). See also Baring-Gould, 82; Opie, 294.

THERE WAS AN OLD WOMAN has been popular ever since the seventeenth century. The Opies note that it had been linked with James II, possibly because it is usually sung to "Lilliburlero," the tune that "danced James II out of three kingdoms" (433). See also Baring-Gould, 50; McMorland, 3; Montgomerie, 127; EFDSS LP101-B1.

TWINKLE, TWINKLE, LITTLE STAR, as the Opies note (397), is one of the best-known poems in the English language. It was written by Jane Taylor (1783-1824) and published under the title of "The Star" in 1806. It quickly passed into oral tradition and has been frequently parodied.

MY HEART LEAPS UP, the famous poem by William Wordsworth (1770-1850), dates from 1807.

THE ANIMALS CAME IN ONE BY ONE, usually titled "One More River," is quite widely known (Best, 102; Brown III, 530; Gullen, 36; Hugill, 99; Peters, 60; Randolph III, 379.

SWEET SINGS THE DONKEY is usually sung as a round (Best, 114; Opie, *Lore*, 176).

IF I HAD A DONKEY circulates in various forms but most of them give the donkey hay or corn instead of a juicy carrot (Baring-Gould, 309; Opie, 153).

IF WISHES WERE HORSES is widely known both as a nursery rhyme and as a proverb (Baring-Gould, 290; Opie, 427; Wilson, 903).

I HAD A LITTLE PONY: Halliwell (216) found the apparent ancestor of this rhyme in a manuscript of about 1630:

    I had a little bonny nagg,
    His name was Dapple Grey
    And he would bring me to an ale-house
    A mile out of my way.

Since then it has become extremely widespread (Baring-Gould, 118; Daiken, 125; Fauset, 131; Fraser, 15; McMorland, 4; Montgomerie, 85; Opie, 143; Ritchie, 55; etc.).

A FARMER WENT TROTTING is somewhat less well known than the previous nursery rhymes (Baring-Gould, 123; Opie, 162).

MY CLOTHING IT WAS ONCE OF THE LINSEY WOOLSEY WEAR appears in De la Mare's *Come Hither* under the title of "Poor Old Horse" (84). See also Kidson and Moffat, 22; Richards, 74.

AS I WAS GOING BY BANBURY CROSS usually begins "Ride a cock-horse to Banbury Cross" and has been popular ever since Ritson printed it in 1784 (21). The Opies discuss the many different versions and surmises about it, and mention that it has been linked to both Queen Elizabeth and Lady Godiva (65). See also Baring-Gould, 247; Daiken, 57; Fraser, 15; Ritchie, 55; etc.

William Cowper (1731-1800) wrote *John Gilpin* in 1793; Anna Sewell (1820-1878) wrote *Black Beauty* in 1877; and Richard Blackmore (1825-1900) wrote *Lorna Doone* in 1869.

IF YOU CHANCE TO WAKE AT MIDNIGHT is part of "A Smuggler's Song" given in *Puck of Pook's Hill*, printed in 1906 (Kipling, 566), and quoted in the Opies' *Oxford Book of Children's Verse* (322).

IT'S NOT THE 'OPPIN' OVER 'EDGES seems to be well known but difficult to identify. It may have originated with a cartoon by John Leech in *Punch*, 21 May 1856, in which a veterinary surgeon tells the owner of a quadruped: "It ain't the 'unting as 'urts 'im. It's the 'ammer, 'ammer, 'ammer along the 'ard 'ighroad."

ONCE THERE WAS A LITTLE KITTY, a poem by Elizabeth Prentiss (1818-1879), appeared in Kenneth Grahame's anthology, *The Cambridge Book of Poetry for Children* (12) under the title of "Kitty." It is sometimes called "Long Time Ago," and sung to the tune of "Coming Through the Rye" (Fowke, *Ring*, 47).

PUSSY CAN SIT BY THE FIRE is from "The Cat That Walked by Himself" in *Just So Stories* (Kipling, 608).

I LOVE LITTLE PUSSY (originally "I like little pussy") is a fairly well-known nursery rhyme often attributed to Jane Taylor (Wiggin, 170), although the Opies doubt that she wrote it (356).

ON THE BANKS OF THE SHANNON is the beginning of a poem titled "The Harper" by Thomas Campbell (1777-1844); it is sometimes called "Old Dog Tray" (Healy III, 138; "Old Favourites," 10 December 1913, et al.).

ROBIN, ROBIN REDBREAST is from a poem, "Robin Redbreast," by William Allingham; it appears in the Opies' *Book of Children's Verse* (219).

THE NORTH WIND DOTH BLOW is a very common nursery rhyme (Baring-Gould, 183; Opie, 426).

DAFFYDOWNDILLY is a very popular rhymed riddle (Baring-Gould, 183; Opie, 141; Taylor, # 652).

RING TING, I WISH I WERE A PRIMROSE is a poem by William Allingham titled "Wishing" and published in the Opies' *Book of Children's Verse* (218).

MY LOVE'S AN ARBUTUS is a poem by A. P. Graves set to a traditional Irish tune (Graves, 143; Stanford, 143).

IF YOU GENTLY TOUCH THE NETTLE appears in the Baring-Goulds' section on "Mother Goose's Charms" (206), and Maggi Peirce knew it from her Irish childhood (17).

THE LASS OF RICHMOND HILL is a poem by Leonard MacNally, set to music by James Hook (Stanford, 52).

NE'ER CAST A CLOUT TILL MAY IS OUT is a fairly well-known proverb (Chambers, 371; Wilson, 106).

LADIES I HAVE GOLDENSILVER is one of the many courting songs in dialogue form. Belden gives many references (506); see also Baring-Gould, 168; Fowke, *Ring*, 122; *Handbook*, 677; etc.

O THE SHAMROCK, THE GREEN IMMORTAL SHAMROCK is one of several songs by Thomas Moore (1779-1852) celebrating Ireland's national emblem (444).

COME BACK TO ERIN, MAVOURNEEN is a famous song by Claribel (Mrs. Charlotte Alington Barnard), published in 1868 (Healy I, 16).

"COME, LITTLE LEAVES" is a children's verse written by George Cooper (1840-1927) and appearing in some early school readers as well as in Wiggin's *Pinafore Palace* (151).

12. I'LL SING YOU A SONG BUT IT'S ALL TOMMYROT

MY LAUGHTER IS OVER is John Oxenford's translation of the well-known Welsh song, "The Ash Grove" (Graves, 141; Stanford, 168).

OFT IN THE STILLY NIGHT is a frequently printed song by Thomas Moore (Hammond, *Moore's Melodies*, 64; Moore, 413; Walton I, 179); and GIVE ME BACK THE WILD FRESHNESS OF MORNING is from a less well-known song, "I Saw from the Beach" (Moore, 451).

PUT ME UPON AN ISLAND WHERE THE GIRLS ARE FEW: This comical ditty about the suffragettes was fairly widely known: Nettl mentions it (215), and Peirce quotes it (23).

I SAW A GIRL COME DOWN A HILL is part of a music-hall routine by Eugene Stratton.

ASSIDY, ASSIDY, SERGEANT MICHAEL CASSIDY: Tony Barker reports a slightly different form of this about "Private Michael Cassidy, V.C." recorded by Jack Norworth on Columbia 2609 and Regal G712 during World War I. He also notes that THE GYPSY WARNED ME was recorded by Violet Lorrie on HMV, and WHERE DO FLIES GO IN THE WINTERTIME by Jack Pleasants on Zono 1970. The latter became a catch phrase, as Ritchie indicates (32).

RUBY LIPS ABOVE THE WATER is from the well-known American song about "Clementine" generally credited to Percy Montross and dating from the 1880s (Best, 25; "Old Favourites," 14 September 1914; et al.).

"OH STAY," THE MAIDEN SAID is a popular college parody of Longfellow's "Excelsior," usually titled "Upidee, Upidah" (Best, 137; Chapple, 88); and UNDER THE SPREADING CHESTNUT TREE is adapted from his "The Village Blacksmith."

LAST NIGHT THERE WERE FOUR MARYS is the best-known stanza of the ancient Scottish ballad "Mary Hamilton," Child 273 (Bronson III, 150; Coffin, 198, 251).

I WAS NOT HALF WORTHY OF YOU appears in *Heart Songs* (Chapple, 84) as "My Douglas! Tender and True," with words credited to Dinah M. Mulock and music to Lady Jane Scott. Mrs. Craik (Diana Maria Mulock) included it in her novel, *John Halifax, Gentleman* (1857).

FAIR AS A LILY is from a fairly familiar American song, "Rosalie, the Prairie Flower" by George F. Root, published in 1885. It is known among traditional singers although rarely reported, and was frequently printed in "Old Favourites" (1 December 1896, et al.).

THERE ARE MANY SAD AND LONELY was a popular song by A. W. French and G. W. Persley titled "Won't You Buy My Pretty Flowers?" (Disher, 215; Nettl, 171).

OH SAY, DON'T YOU KNOW HOW A LONG TIME AGO stems from the well-known song about "The Babes in the Wood." Originally a long ballad, it was entered in the *Stationer's Register* in 1595 under the title, "The Norfolk Gentleman, His Will and Testament. . ." and may have been based on an old play. It appeared on various English, Irish, and Scottish broadsides and survived in tradition in both Britain and America (Dean-Smith, 51; Laws, 290). However, it is better known as a short lament which turns up in nursery-rhyme books and collections of children's lore (Baring-Gould, 148; Howard, 273; Halliwell, 27; McMorland, 73; Peirce, 48; etc.).

THERE WERE THREE JEWS CALLED PATRIARCHS is a widely known children's song still popular in summer camps (Best, 133; Fowke, 98; Fraser, 17; McMorland, 80; etc.).

POOR OLD ROBINSON CRUSOE is an English nursery rhyme that does not seem to have crossed the Atlantic, although it has been heard on music-hall stages and printed in songsters since the eighteenth century (Baring-Gould, 146; Opie, 373).

LET ERIN REMEMBER is one of the most frequently printed of Thomas Moore's songs (Graves, 29; Hammond, *Moore's Melodies*, 28; Moore, 431; Stanford, 112; Walton II, 54; Wehman, 13).

OH LIST TO THE TALE OF A POOR IRISH HARPER is the

opening of "The Bard of Armagh," a popular Irish folk song whose tune was appropriated for the American cowboy song, "The Streets of Laredo" (De la Mare, 83; Hayward, 10; Hughes II, 1; Healy I, 128; O'Conor, 50; Walton I, 178; Wehman, 13).

AND HE WALKS WITH ME comes from a religious song, "In the Garden," composed by C. Austin Mills.

I WORE MY PAPPY'S PANTS is a parody of "The Holy City" by Stephen Adams which became popular in 1892. The parody echoes its refrain of "Jerusalem, Jerusalem."

WE'VE GOT A NAVY, THE BRITISH NAVY is from a song "The Lads in Navy Blue" (Pulling, 80).

WE'RE SOLDIERS OF THE QUEEN, M'LADS is a patriotic British song that Leslie Stuart wrote in 1891; it was used as a recruiting song in the Boer War (MacInnes, 79; Pulling, 79; Winstock, 253).

I AM A FRIAR OF ORDERS GREY was written by John O'Keeffe (1747-1833) for a musical play, "Merry Sherwood." It was described as "a ballad supposed to have been written in the twelfth century" (Hoagland, 348).

OF PRIESTS WE CAN OFFER A CHARMING VARIETY, the story of "Father O'Flynn," is the most famous song of the well-known Irish songwriter Alfred Perceval Graves (1846-1931). It has been frequently reprinted (Graves, 76; Hoagland, 555; O'Conor, 129; Wehman, 59; "Old Favourites," 17 March 1915); and translated into other languages. In his autobiography, *To Return to All That*, Graves notes that Father O'Flynn was patterned on Father Michael Walsh of County Kerry.

ALL ALONG OF DIRTINESS is a fragment of a Kipling song, "The 'Eathen" (451).

I'LL SING YOU A SONG BUT IT'S ALL TOMMYROT is patterned on "Six Miles from Bangor to Donaghadee" and has a variety of comical verses. Maggi Peirce remembered the stanza about Miss Brown (4), and Mrs. Fraser quotes a verse beginning "How would you like to be me?" (182).

LOUD ROARED THE DREADFUL THUNDER is from "The Bay

of Biscay O" by Andrew Cherry (Stanford, 27).

WHEN YOU CLIMB OUT OF BED WITH A FROWSLY HEAD is part of a poem accompanying "How the Camel Got Its Hump" in *Just So Stories*, first published in 1902 (Kipling, 604); and IF YOU STOP TO THINK WHAT YOUR WAGES WILL BE is from a poem entitled "Mary's Son" (Kipling, 373). MAGGIE MY WIFE AT FIFTY is from another Kipling piece, "The Betrothal" (47); the same theme was popularized by Harry B. Smith and Victor Herbert as "A Woman Is Only a Woman" in 1905.

IN CARRICKMACROSS AND CROSSMAGLEN expresses the distrust of the farming folk for the dealers in the towns. Sam Hanna Bell (89) notes this attitude: "Most Ulster people have heard the heart-cry of the deluded farmer:
> "'Twas the daling-men
> From Crossmaglen
> Put whiskey in my tae!"

13. WHERE THE ALLEYMAN WON'T CATCH ME

OH, MY FATHER AND MOTHER ARE IRISH is a little ditty sometimes used for a singing game in both Britain and America (Brown I, 107; Rutherford, 70; Shaw, 5).

MY MOTHER HAS TOLD ME THAT WHEN I WAS BORN is from "Come Back, Paddy Reilly, to Ballyjamesduff" by Percy French (1854-1920) that was published in 1912 (Healy, *French*, 24; Top Rank International 25/020-A1).

THE DEAR LITTLE SHAMROCK is from a verse by Andrew Cherry (1762-1812) that appears in various Irish songsters (Healy I, 20; O'Conor, 112; Walton II, 110).

H, A, DOUBLE R, I, GAN SPELLS HARRIGAN is a popular song by George M. Cohan (1878-1942), written for a musical, "Fifty Miles from Boston," 1907.

LITTLE INDIAN, SIOUX, OR CROW is from a poem, "Foreign Children," by R. L. Stevenson: it appeared in his *Child's Garden of Verse*, 1885.

FATHER AND MOTHER AND ME is from a Kipling poem, "We and They" (768). The last two lines in the original run:
>But — would you believe it? — They look upon We
>As only a sort of They!

COCK A DOODLE, COCK A DOODLE is the bagpipe tune, "Cock of the North."

YOU MAY TALK ABOUT YOUR KING'S GUARDS is the chorus of "The South Down Militia" by Peadar Kearney (1890-1940), who also wrote the Irish national anthem. See Behan, 86; Graham, 13; Hammond, 40; O'Boyle, 52; Walton I, 16.

BAD LUCK TO THIS MARCHING is from a poem Charles Lever (1806-1872) incorporated in his novel *Charles O'Malley*; it was set to the air of "Paddy O'Carroll" (Behan, 6; Lover, 206; Hoagland, 440).

THEY STOLE LITTLE BRIDGET is from a poem, "The Fairies," by William Allingham, said to have been inspired by a Jacobite verse:
>'Tis up the rocky mountain and down the mossy glen
>We darena gang a-milking for Charlie and his men.

Daiken reports a stanza as part of a game played in County Down (155), and the Kings give it as a skipping rhyme (27). For the full text, see Hoagland, 509; or Opie, *Children's Verse*, 215.

THE STOLEN CHILD by W. B. Yeats (1865-1939) appears in Hoagland's *1000 Years of Irish Poetry* (594).

OH, THE MOON SHINES BRIGHT ON CHARLIE CHAPLIN is a widely known World War I rhyme parodying the 1907 popular song, "Red Wing." Brophy gives it as a soldiers' song (38), but it has had a longer life as a children's ditty. Charlie Chaplin is extremely popular with the juvenile set: Abrahams gives half a dozen other Chaplin rhymes used for skipping (25), and this one is still in oral circulation in Ireland, England, and Australia (Peirce, 22; Opie, *Lore*, 109; Ritchie, 23; Shaw, 52; Turner, 108).

The Opies found a similar KAISER BILL rhyme in England (*Lore*, 98).

LITTLE TIRPITZ HAS LOST HIS SHIPS parodies "Mary Had a Little Lamb"; and HOW THEY GIGGLED, HOW THEY LAUGHED parodies John Reid's "Granny's Old Arm Chair."

I WANT TO GO HOME: Dolph tells us that Lieutenant Gitz Rice, a Canadian, wrote the first version of this song and later the Americans adopted it (99). His version runs:

> I want to go home! I want to go home!
> The bullets they whistle, the cannons they roar;
> I don't want to stay here any more.
> Take me over the sea
> Where the Germans they can't get at me.
> Oh, my! I'm too young to die!
> I want to go home.

Brophy, whose version is like Alice's, does not name a composer but notes: "This was one of the most famous of war songs. It marks the first disillusionments of the 1914 volunteer when he discovered that war was not romantic and that the Germans were not subhuman" (60).

WHEN THIS RUDDY WAR IS OVER has been popular ever since the American Civil War in slightly different forms. Dolph has it as "cruel war" (339), Brophy as "blasted war" (63), and Hopkins as "bloody war" (103). It goes to the tune of George F. Root's "Just Before the Battle, Mother."

OH, IT'S A LOVELY WAR originated with the British Tommies (Pulling, 83) but was soon picked up by the Americans (Dolph, 143). It later provided the title for an English musical.

IF YOU WANT THE SERGEANT-MAJOR and HANGING ON THE OLD BARBED WIRE come from a song well known to British, American, and Canadian servicemen (Brophy, 72; Dolph, 87; Hopkins, 90; Niles, 59). It dates from the First World War when it was known as "The Old Barbed Wire."

FORM FOURS TO THE RIGHT is a fragment from "Old King Cole," originally a nursery rhyme dating back at least to 1708 (Opie, 34) and rewritten by soldiers (Dolph, 45; Hopkins, 96). It is also popular among children as a camp song and among rugby players in a bawdy parody.

OLD SOLDIERS NEVER DIE: Brophy gives this as a British army song to the air of "Kind Thoughts Can Never Die" (67), and Ritchie notes: "In the side-streets in 1919 small boys playing at soldiers were greatly given to marching and bawling out: 'Old soldiers never die. . .'" (30).

WHERE ARE THE BOYS OF THE VILLAGE TONIGHT? is from a music-hall song by George Lashwood written in 1914 (Pulling, 39).

PACK UP YOUR TROUBLES is by George Asap and Felix Powell, published in 1915 (Hopkins, 21); and KEEP THE HOME FIRES BURNING is by Lena Guilbert Ford and Ivor Novello, 1915. Both were very popular and outlived the war period.

GOOD-BYE-EE, DON'T CRY-EE by Harry Tate is less familiar but must have been very well known at the time, for it has survived in various parodies. Rutherford gives one from Birtley (114) and Shaw has two from Liverpool, including the one about the flu that Alice quotes later (40, 106).

TAKE ME BACK TO DEAR OLD BLIGHTY by A. J. Mills, Fred Godfrey, and Bennett Scott was published in 1916 and became an instant hit. Blighty was soldiers' slang for England in the sense of home. As Brophy notes, "In this one word was gathered all the soldier's homesickness and affection and war-weariness. . . . Blighty to the soldier was a sort of faerie, a paradise which he could faintly remember, a never-never land" (99).

O MY LILY O: Compare "The Orange Lily-O" in Hayward's *Ulster Songs and Ballads*, 116, and O Lochlainn's *Irish Street Ballads*, 140.

ON THE GREEN GRASSY SLOPES OF THE BOYNE is a popular Orange song commemorating King William's victory at the battle of the Boyne in 1690 (Graham, 22; Harbison, 120).

UP COMES A MAN WITH A SHOVEL IN HIS HAND: Maggi Peirce also knew this in her Ulster childhood (14), and Betty Messenger has a similar verse (163).

HOLD THE FORT FOR BALFOUR'S COMING is one of the many parodies of the gospel hymn Philip P. Bliss published in 1870. For the history of the song and its many versions, see *Hold the Fort!* by Paul J. Scheips. Arthur James Balfour (1848-1930) was British foreign secretary during World War I.

THE WIDE, WIDE WORLD is by Elizabeth Wetherell (1819-1885), *LITTLE WOMEN* by Louisa May Alcott (1832-1880), *WHAT KATY DID* by Susan Coolidge (1835-1905), and *TOM SAWYER* by Mark Twain (1835-1910). ANGELA BRAZIL wrote school stories such as

The Fifth Form and *The Darling of the School*; BESSIE BUNTER appeared in a comic book: the female counterpart of the better-known Billy Bunter.

THE YANKS ARE COMING OVER parodies "Over There," George M. Cohan's best-known song, which was first performed in New York in 1917.

MADEMOISELLE FROM ARMENTIÈRES is probably the most famous song of World War I (Dolph, 83; Hopkins, 26; Niles, 15), but it and its many parodies have had a longer life among children. The Opies note: "In the west of Scotland they chant, count out, or play two-balls, and in Swansea, skip to, their own version" (*Lore*, 92); and other versions are known elsewhere (Ritchie, 26, Shaw, 60).

MR. PUSSYFOOT, BOW WOW is a ditty inspired by American prohibition, probably based on an army song, "We'll Drink Old England Dry" (Winstock, 184).

ARAWANA ON ME HONOUR is from a music-hall song by Jack Drislane and Theodore F. Morse, published in 1906.

Publications Cited

(Irish items are asterisked)

Abrahams, Roger. *Jump-Rope Rhymes: A Dictionary*. Austin: Univ. of Texas Press, 1969.

Abrahams, Roger, and Lois Rankin. *Counting-Out Rhymes: A Dictionary*. Austin: Univ. of Texas Press, 1980.

Anderson, Hugh. *Time Out of Mind: Simon McDonald of Creswick*. Melbourne, Australia: National Press, 1974.

Baring-Gould, William S., and Ceil Baring-Gould. *The Annotated Mother Goose*. New York: Clarkson N. Potter, 1962.

*Behan, Dominic. *Ireland Sings*. London: Essex, 1965.

*Bell, Sam Hanna. *Erin's Orange Lily: Ulster Customs and Folklore*. London: Dennis Dobson, 1956.

Best, Dick, and Beth Best. *Song Fest*. New York: Oliver Durrell, 1948.

Bolton, Henry C. *The Counting-Out Rhymes of Children*. London: Elliot Stack, 1888.

Botkin, B. A. *A Treasury of American Folklore*. New York: Crown, 1954.

─────. *The American Play-Party Song*. New York: Frederick Ungar, 1957.

─────. *A Treasury of Western Folklore*. New York, Crown, 1951.

*Brady, Eilís. *All In! All In! A Selection of Dublin Children's Traditional Street-Games with Rhymes and Music*. Dublin: Comhairle Bhéaloideas Éireann, 1975.

Bronson, Bertrand. *The Traditional Tunes of the Child Ballads*. 4 vols. Princeton: Princeton Univ. Press, 1959-1972.

Brophy, John, and Eric Partridge. *Songs and Slang of the British Soldier 1914-1918*. London: Eric Partridge, 1930.

Brown, Frank C. *The Frank C. Brown Collection of North Carolina Folklore*. 7 vols. Durham: Duke Univ. Press, 1952.

Browne, Ray B. *The Alabama Folk Lyric: A Study in Origins and Media of Dissemination*. Bowling Green: Bowling Green University Popular Press, 1979.

Buchan, Norman, and Peter Hall. *The Scottish Folksinger*. London & Glasgow: Collins, 1973.

*Buck, Alan M. *When I Was a Boy in Ireland*. New York: Lothrop, Lee & Shepard, 1936.

Chambers, Robert. *Popular Rhymes of Scotland*. 1841; 4th ed. London & Edinburgh: W. & R. Chambers, 1870.

Chapple, Joe Mitchell. *Heart Songs*. Cleveland & New York: World, 1950.

Child, Francis James. *The English and Scottish Popular Ballads*. 5 vols. Boston & New York: Houghton, Mifflin, 1882-1898.

Christie, Agatha. *Mrs. McGinty's Dead*. London: Collins, 1952; rpt. 1972.

Coffin, Tristram P., and Roger DeV. Renwick. *The British Traditional Ballad in North America*. Austin & London: Univ. of Texas Press, 1977.

Cosbey, Robert C. *All in Together, Girls: Skipping Songs from Regina, Saskatchewan*. Regina: Univ. of Regina, 1980.

*Daiken, Leslie. *Children's Games Throughout the Year*. New York & London: Batsford, 1949.

*—————. *Out Goes She! Dublin Street Rhymes*. Dublin: Dolmen Press, 1963.

Dean, M. C. *Flying Cloud*. Virginia, MI: Quickprint, 1922.

Dean-Smith, Margaret. *A Guide to English Folk Song Collections 1822-1952*. Liverpool: Univ. of Liverpool and English Folk Dance and Song Society, 1954.

De la Mare, Walter. *Come Hither*. New York: Knopf, 1923; rpt. Toronto: Longmans Canada, 1960.

Disher, Maurice William. *Victorian Song*. London: Phoenix House, 1955.

Dolph, Edward Arthur. *Sound Off! Soldier Songs from the Revolution to World War II*. New York: Farrar & Rinehart, 1949.

Douglas, Norman. *London Street Games*. 1916; London: Chatto & Windus, 1931.

Elder, J. D. *Song Games from Trinidad and Tobago*. Philadelphia: American Folklore Society, 1965.

Emrich, Duncan. *The Nonsense Book of Riddles, Rhymes, Tongue Twisters, Puzzles and Jokes from American Folklore*. New York: Four Winds, 1970.

Emrich, Marion V., and George Korson. *The Child's Book of Folklore*. New York: Dial Press, 1947.

Evans, Patricia. *Rimbles*. New York: Doubleday, 1961.

Fauset, Arthur Huff. *Folklore from Nova Scotia*. New York: American Folklore Society, 1931.

Ford, Robert. *Children's Rhymes, Games, Songs, Stories*. Paisley: Alexander Gardner, 1904.

Fowke, Edith. *Sally Go Round the Sun*. Toronto: McClelland & Stewart, 1969.

—————. *The Penguin Book of Canadian Folk Songs*. Harmondsworth: Penguin, 1973.

—————. *Ring Around the Moon*. Toronto: McClelland & Stewart, 1977.

—————. *Traditional Singers and Songs from Ontario*. Hatboro, PA: Folklore Associates, 1965.

Fowke, Edith, and Alan Mills. *Canada's Story in Song*. Toronto: W. J. Gage, 1960.

Fraser, Amy Stewart. *Dae Ye Min' Lang Syne? A Pot Pourri of Games, Rhymes and Plots of Scottish Childhood*. London: Routledge & Kegan Paul, 1975.

Frey, Hugo. *Canada Sings*. New York: Robbins, 1935.

Gammond, Peter. *Best Musical Hall and Variety Songs*. London: Wolfe, 1972.

*Gailey, Alan. *Irish Folk Drama*. Cork: Mercier, 1969.

*Ghallchoir, Meav Bean Ui. "The Duke of Spain and My Sister Jane: Some Children's Games from Dublin." *Ceol*, 4(1981), 110-14.

*Gomme, Alice B. *The Traditional Games of England, Scotland, and Ireland*. 2 vols. London: David Nutt, 1894; rpt. New York: Dover, 1964.

*Graham, Neil. *The Orange Songster*. Glasgow: James S. Kerr, n.d.

Grahame, Kenneth. *The Cambridge Book of Poetry for Children*. Cambridge: Univ. Press, 1916; 1932.

*Graves, Alfred Perceval. *The Celtic Song Book*. N.p.: Ernest Benn, 1928.

Gregor, Walter. "Children's Amusements." *Folk-Lore Journal*, 4(1886), 132-57.

Gullen, F. Doreen. *Traditional Number Rhymes and Games*. London, Univ. of London Press, 1950.

Halliwell, James Orchard. *The Nursery Rhymes of England*. Percy Society Publications, 1842. 1843 edition cited.

*Hammond, David. *Songs of Belfast*. Dublin: Gilbert Dalton, 1978.

*—————. *Moore's Melodies*. Dublin: Gilbert Dalton, 1979.

Handbook: See Ó Súilleabháin.

*Harbison, Robert. *No Surrender: An Ulster Childhood*. London: Faber & Faber, 1960.

*Hayward, Richard. *Ireland Calling*. Glasgow: Mozart Alan, n.d.

*—————. *Ulster Songs and Ballads of the Town and Country*. London: Duckworth, 1925.

*Healy, James N. *Old Irish Street Ballads*. 3 vols. Cork: Mercier, 1967-1969.

*—————. *Percy French and His Songs*. Cork: Mercier, 1966.

*Hoagland, Kathleen. *1000 Years of Irish Poetry*. New York: Grosset & Dunlop, 1962.

Holbrook, David. *Children's Games*. London: Gordon Fraser, 1957.

Hopkins, Anthony. *Songs from the Front and Rear: Canadian Servicemen's Songs from the Second World War*. Edmonton: Hurtig, 1979.

Hornby, John. *The Joyous Book of Singing Games*. Leeds, Glasgow, & Belfast: E. J. Arnold, n.d.

Howard, Dorothy. *Dorothy's World*. Englewood Cliffs, NJ: Prentice-Hall, 1977.

Hudson, Arthur Palmer. *Folksongs of Mississippi*. Chapel Hill: Univ. of North Carolina Press, 1936.

*Hughes, Herbert. *Irish Country Songs*. 4 vols. London: Boosey & Hawkes, 1909-1936.

Hugill, Stan. *Shanties from the Seven Seas*. London: Routledge & Kegan Paul, 1961.

―――――. *Shanties and Sailors' Songs*. New York: Praeger, 1969.

Hunter, Molly. *A Sound of Chariots*. London: Collins, 1975.

Ingelow, Jean. *Poems*. Vol. 1. London: Longmans Green, 1882.

Johnson, James. *The Scots Musical Museum*. 1788; 1853; rpt. Hatboro, PA: Folklore Associates, 1962.

Journal of the Irish Folk Song Society, London, 1904-1939.

*Joyce, James. *Portrait of the Artist as a Young Man*. New York: Viking, 1944.

Justus, May. *The Complete Peddler's Pack*. Knoxville: Univ. of Tennessee Press, 1957.

Kidson, Frank, and Alfred Moffat. *A Garland of English Folk-Songs*. London: Ascherberg, Hopword & Crew, n.d.

Kidson, Frank, and Martin Shaw. *Songs of Britain*. London: Boosey & Co., 1913.

King, Madge, and Robert King. *Street Games of North Shields Children*. 2nd series. Tynemouth: Priory Press, 1930.

Kipling, Rudyard. *Rudyard Kipling's Verse*. Definitive Edition. London: Hodder & Stoughton, 1966.

Knapp, Mary, and Herbert Knapp. *One Potato, Two Potato: The Secret Education of American Children*. New York: Norton, 1976.

Langstaff, John, and Carol Langstaff. *Shimmy Shimmy Coke-Ca-Pop! A Collection of City Children's Street Games and Rhymes*. Garden City: Doubleday, 1973.

Laws, J. Malcolm, Jr. *American Ballads from British Broadsides*. Philadelphia: American Folklore Society, 1957.

*Lover, Samuel, ed. *Poems of Ireland*. London: Ward, Lock, 1858.

Lowenstein, Wendy. *Shocking! Shocking! Shocking!* Victoria, Australia: Fish & Chip Press, 1974.

*Lynch, Geraldine. "The Lore of a Wicklow Schoolgirl." *Béaloideas*, 45-47(1977-79), 46-62.

MacInnes, Colin. *Sweet Saturday Night*. London: MacGibbon & Kee, 1967.

McKibbin, Jack. "Childhood Days in Dundonald." *Ulster Folklife*, 26(1980), 41-54.

McMorland, Alison. *The Funny Family*. London: Ward Lock Educational, 1978.

MacNabb, Iaian. *Night at Eenie: The Bairns' Parnassus.* Warlingham, Surrey: Samson Press, 1932.

Mattfield, Julius. *Variety Musical Cavalcade*. Englefield Cliffs, NJ: Prentice-Hall, 1962.

*Meek, Bill. *Songs of the Irish in America*. Dublin: Gilbert Dalton, 1978.

*Messenger, Betty. *Picking Up the Linen Threads*. Austin & London: Univ. of Texas Press, 1978.

Miscellanea of the Rymour Club. 3 vols. Edinburgh: John Knox's House, 1906-1911.

Montgomerie, Norah, and William Montgomerie. *The Hogarth Book of Scottish Nursery Rhymes*. London: Hogarth, 1964.

*Moore. *The Poetical Works of Thomas Moore*. Edinburgh: William P. Nimmo, 1872.

Morris, Alton. *Folksongs of Florida*. Gainesville: Univ. of Florida Press, 1950.

*Morton, Robin. *Folksongs Sung in Ulster*. Cork: Mercier, 1970.

Nettl, Reginald. *Seven Centuries of Popular Song*. London: Phoenix, 1956.

Newell, William Wells. *Games and Songs of American Children*. New York: Harper, 1903; rpt. New York: Dover, 1963.

Nicholson, Edward W. B. *Golspie: Contributions to Its Folklore*. London: David Nutt, 1897.

Niles, John J., and Douglas S. Moore. *Songs My Mother Never Taught Me*. New York: Gold Label, 1929.

Northall, G. F. *English Folk Rhymes*. London: Kegan Paul, Trench, Trubner & Co., 1892.

*O Boyle, Cathal. *Songs of County Down*. Dublin: Gilbert Dalton, 1979.

Occomore, David, and Philip Spratley. *Bushes & Briars*. Loughton, Essex: Caxton House, 1979.

*O'Conor, Manus. *Irish Com-All-Ye's*. New York: Lipkind, 1901.

Ogilvie, Mary I. *A Scottish Childhood*. Oxford: Gerge Ronald, 1952.

*O'Hare, Colette. *What Do You Feed Your Donkey On? Rhymes from a Belfast Childhood*. London: Collins, 1978.

*O'Keeffe. Daniel D. *The First Book of Irish Ballads*. Cork: Mercier, 1955.

"Old Favourites." Column in *The Family Herald and Weekly Star*, Montreal, 1895-1968. Indexed in *Canadian Folk Music Journal*, 7(1979), 29-56.

*O Lochlainn, Colm. *Irish Street Ballads*. Dublin: Sign of the Three Candles, 1939.

—————. *More Irish Street Ballads*. Dublin: Sign of the Three Candles, 1965.

Opie, Iona, and Peter Opie. *The Oxford Dictionary of Nursery Rhymes*. Oxford: Oxford Univ. Press, 1951.

—————, and —————. *Children's Games in Street and Playground*. Oxford: Oxford Univ. Press, 1969.

—————, and —————. *A Family Book of Nursery Rhymes*. New York: Oxford Univ. Press, 1964. (Same as *The Puffin Book of Nursery Rhymes* in England.)

—————, and —————. *I Saw Esau: Traditional Rhymes of Youth*. London: Williams & Norgate, 1947.

—————, and —————. *The Lore and Language of Schoolchildren*. Oxford: Oxford Univ. Press, 1959.

—————, and —————. *The Oxford Book of Children's Verse*. Oxford: Oxford Univ. Press, 1973.

—————, and —————. *The Oxford Nursery Rhyme Book*. Oxford: Oxford Univ. Press, 1960.

*Ó Súilleabháin, Seán. *A Handbook of Irish Folklore*. London: Herbert Jenkins, 1942. (Cited as *Handbook*.)

Palmer, Roy. *The Rambling Soldier*. Harmondsworth: Penguin, 1977.

*Peirce, Maggi Kerr. *Keep the Kettle Boiling. These rhymes, chants, songs, etc. are remembered from my childhood in Northern Ireland*. N.p.: Author, 1979.

Peters, Harry B. *Folk Songs out of Wisconsin*. Madison: State Historical Society of Wisconsin, 1977.

Pinto, V. de Sola, and A. E. Rodway. *The Common Muse*. London: Chatto & Windus, 1957.

Pope-Hennessy, James. *Queen Mary (1867-1953)*. London: George Allen & Unwin, c. 1959.

The Presbyterian Book of Praise. Oxford: University Press, 1901.

Pulling, Christopher. *They Were Singing*. London: Harrap, 1952.

Randolph, Vance, and Floyd C. Shoemaker. *Ozark Folksongs*. 4 vols. Columbia: Historical Society of Missouri, 1946-1955.

Richards, Sam, and Tish Stubbs. *The English Folksinger*. London: Collins, 1979.

Richardson, Ethel Park. *American Mountain Songs*. New York: Greenberg, 1927.

Ritchie, James T. R. *The Singing Street*. Edinburgh & London: Oliver & Boyd, 1964.

—————. *The Golden City*. Edinburgh & London: Oliver & Boyd, 1965.

[Ritson, Joseph.] *Gammer Gurton's Garland*. 1784; 1810; rpt. Norwood, PA: Norwood Editions, 1973.

Rutherford, Frank. *All the Way to Pennywell. Children's Rhymes of the North East*. Durham: Univ. of Durham Institute of Education, 1971.

Rymour: See *Miscellanea of the Rymour Club*.

Sandburg, Carl. *The American Songbag*. NY: Harcourt, Brace, 1927.

Scheips, Paul J. *Hold the Fort!* Washington: Smithsonian Institution Press, 1971.

Seeger, Pete. *The Bells of Rhymney*. New York: Oak, 1964.

Shaw, Frank. *You Know Me Anty Nelly? Liverpool Children's Rhymes*. London: Wolfe, 1970.

Solomon, Jack, and Olivia Solomon. *Zickary Zan*. University: Univ. of Alabama, 1980.

Spaeth, Sigmund. *A History of Popular Music in America*. New York: Random House, 1948.

Stanford, C. V., and Geoffrey Shaw. *The New National Song Book*. London: Boosey, 1918.

Sutton-Smith, Brian. *The Folkgames of Children*. Austin: Univ. of Texas Press, 1972.

Taylor, Archer. *English Riddles from Oral Tradition*. Berkeley & Los Angeles: Univ. of California Press, 1951.

Thompson, Flora. *Lark Rise to Candleford*. London: Oxford, 1943; Harmondsworth: Penguin, 1973.

Those Dusty Bluebells. Kilmarnock, Scotland: Cumnock Academy, 1965.

Turner, Ian. *Cinderella Dressed in Yella*. New York: Taplinger, 1972.

Walton's New Treasury of Irish Songs and Ballads. 2 vols. Dublin: Walton's, 1966, 1968.

Watters, Eugene, and Matthew Murtagh. *Infinite Varieties: Dan Lowrey's Music Hall 1878-1897*. Dublin: Gill & MacMillan, 1975.

*Wehman. *Six Hundred and Seventeen Irish Songs and Ballads*. New York: Wehman, n.d.

Wiggin, Kate D., and Nora A. Smith. *Pinafore Palace*. 1907; rpt. Plainview, NY: Books for Libraries Press, 1972.

Wilson, F. P. *The Oxford Dictionary of English Proverbs*. 3rd ed. Oxford: Oxford Univ. Press, 1970.

Winstock, Lewis. *Songs and Music of the Redcoats*. Harrisburg, PA: Stackpole, 1970.

Withers, Carl. *Rocket in My Pocket*. New York: Holt, Rinehart & Winston, 1948.

*Zimmerman, Georges-Denis. *Songs of Irish Rebellion*. Hatboro, PA: Folklore Associates, 1967.

Records Cited

(Irish items are asterisked)

*Arfolk SB 307. *Irish Folk Music*. Ted Furey.

*Arts Council of Northern Ireland LPS 3018. *Green Peas and Barley O. Children's street songs and rhymes from Belfast*, 1974.

Caedmon TC 1225. *Animal Songs*. The Folk Songs of Britain, Vol. X. Ed. Peter Kennedy and Alan Lomax.

*Claddagh CC9. *An Aill Bain (The White Rock)*. Sean Ac Donnca, 1971.

*Columbia KL 204. *Irish Folk Songs*. Columbia World Library of Folk and Primitive Music, Vol. 1. Ed. Seamus Ennis and Alan Lomax.

Columbia KL 206. *English Folk Songs*. Columbia World Library of Folk and Primitive Music, Vol. 3. Ed. Peter Kennedy and Alan Lomax.

EFDSS LP 101. *William Kimber*.

*Folk Legacy FSE 8. *Peg Clancy Power, Carrick-on-Suir, County Tipperary, Eire*, 1962.

*Folk Lyric FL 113. *Finnegans Wake and Other Irish Folksongs*. Dominic Behan, 1958.

Folktracks FSB 027. *The Frog and the Mouse: Songs of Diversion*, 1975.

Folktracks FSC 30-201. *One-Two-Three-A-Loopah* (Devon children), 1975.

Folktracks FSC 45-181. *Ipetty-Sippetty: Scottish Children's Games and Rhymes*, 1978.

*Folktracks FSA 60-072. *The Doffin Mistress: Street Songs and Games of Belfast*. Collected by Hugh Quinn in the 1890s; issued in 1975.

Folktracks FSB 60-516. *The Deadly Wars*, 1979.

Folkways 2005. *American Folk Songs Sung by the Seegers*, 1957.

*Folkways 3003. *The Orangemen of Ulster*. Recorded by Samuel B. Charters, 1961.

Folkways 3565. *The Elliots of Birtley*, 1962.

Folkways 7003. *1, 2, 3, and a Zing Zing Zing*. Recorded by Tony Schwartz, 1953.

Folkways 7029. *Skip Rope Games*. Recorded by Pete Seeger, 1955.

*Folkways 8501. *The Singing Streets: Childhood Memories of Ireland and Scotland*. Ewan MacColl and Dominic Behan, 1958.

*Intercord Xenophon Int. 181.002. *The 2nd Irish Folk Festival on Tour*, 1975.

Leader LED 2111. *Our Side of the Baulk*. Walter Pardon, 1977.

Prestige International 13004. *The Best of Ewan MacColl*.

*Rex 15064. "The Irish Schoolmaster" and "Darling Jimmy," Belfast Girl Singers (78 rpm).

*Top Rank International 25/020. *Margaret Barry*.

Topic 12TS324. *Round Rye Bay for More*. Johnny Doughty, 1977.

*Tradition TLP 1004. *The Lark in the Morning. Songs and Dances from the Irish Countryside*. Collected by Diane Hamilton.

*Tradition TLP 1034. *So Early in the Morning. Irish Children's Traditional Songs, Rhymes, and Games*. Collected by Diane Hamilton.

Wattle Archive Series 2. *Australian Traditional Singers and Musicians of Victoria*. Collected by members of the Folklore Society of Victoria, 1963.

Songs Known by James Joyce

M. J. C. Hodgart and Mabel Worthington wrote *James Joyce: Song in the Works of James Joyce* (Philadelphia: Temple University, 1959), and they indicate that Joyce quoted or referred to the following songs and rhymes that Alice knew in her childhood:

The Absent-Minded Beggar
Amo Amas
Babes in the Wood
Barney O'Hea
Boys of the Old Brigade
Brian O'Linn
Caller Herrin'
Clap Hands
Cockles and Mussels
Come Back, Paddy Reilly
Come Back to Erin
Daffydowndilly
The Dear Little Shamrock
A Diller, A Dollar
The Farmer in the Dell
Father O'Flynn
The Garden Where the Praties Grow
God Save Ireland
Going to St. Ives
Good-Bye-ee
The Grand Old Duke of York
The Happy Land
Harrigan
The Holy City
Hooligan's Christmas Cake
I Know Where I'm Going
The Irish Jaunting Car
I Saw from the Beach

Jenny Jones
Johnny Come Down from Hilo
Let Erin Remember
Little Polly Flinders
Mademoiselle from Armentières
The Mulberry Bush
My Love's an Arbutus
Nae Luck About the House
Nuts in May
Oft in the Stilly Night
One, Two, Buckle My Shoe
Over There
Pack Up Your Troubles
Poor Old Robinson Crusoe
Ride a Cock Horse
Ring-a-ring-a-Roses
Rio Grande
Scotland's Burning
She Sells Sea Shells
There Is a Boarding House
This Is the Way the Ladies Ride
This Little Piggy
Tipperary
Tramp, Tramp, Tramp
Twinkle, Twinkle, Little Star
Two Little Girls in Blue
The West's Awake
The Whistlin' Thief

Index of Titles and First Lines

250